Jo

THE IRISHMAN

Mine & My Fathers Truth

About

JFK Conspiracy & Hoffa

Disappearance

SEAN COLLINS

First Published in the US in 2017 by Amazon and Kindle.

The Writers Guild of America, issues this certificate to:

John Francis Sullivan Jr

For the Fictitious Novel

"JOHN FRANCIS"

"THE IRISHMAN"

ISBN 9781521954409 Date Registered on 6/27/2017

The author has made every effort to clear all copyright permissions, but where this has been possible and amendments are required, the author will be pleased to make and necessary arrangements at the earliest opportunity.

Some of the names and facts have been changed in this novel for the sake of anonymity to protect others.

Introduction to the Author

John Francis "The Irishman" is based on true story's and real events. There is information in this book that is fictitious mostly for the need of anonymity for others.

This novel is the first of five that will provide inside information on crime and corruption in Providence RI. Most of this book is based on the personal knowledge of John F. Sullivan Jr aka Sean Collins. These experiences also include personal conversations he had with the many people who were allegedly involved in organized crime and corrupt Rhode Island politicians. These conversations and experiences took place from the 1960s through the early 2000's. He had personal relationships with many of these people because of his Dad's association in organized crime and politics on the city and state in Rhode Island and reached as high as the Nixon White House.

The JFK and Hoffa information came from talks he had with his Dad over the years. Most of the real personal information came over the last 18 months of Dad's life while suffering with cancer. Personal meeting's Jr had with JFK in 1960, and Jimmy Hoffa numerous times in the 1970s. Frank Sheeran, and Russell Bufalino also discussed events in 1974 and in 1978 in Watch Hill RI in which Jr was present.

Numerous personal conversations Jr also had with Raymond Patriarca Sr. over the years during his nearly daily visits to the "Office" on Federal Hill. While working on the emergency truck for the City of Providence, with fellow workers Anthony Melise, and Anthony, "Blackjack" Del Santo.

Dedication

I am dedicating this novel to my Grandmother, "Catherine Collins Sullivan" who raised me from the age of five when my parents divorced. Nana was 70 years young when I went to live with her on Smith Hill in Providence RI. I was the youngest boy and the last to carry on the family name.

Nana was certainly an old school Irish Grandmother. She raised me in her native Irish way of how they made young boys into good strong men with solid foundations that would carry them throughout their lives. At a very young age she would talk to me about this young boy that she knew from her childhood. She would tell me that I reminded her of him, we both had so much energy and this inquisitive nature and fearlessness about ourselves that set us apart from other children. She also said that we both were what the Irish called was The Irish Alpha Male. The Irish Alpha Male was looked at as the leader of his clan or family structure, it was his responsibility to be the strong protective one of his clan. Nothing like the American Alpha Male that was full of himself and thought he was a tough guy and nine times out of ten just a bully.

Nana went on to say that there are only two different kinds of people in this world so keep it simple, there are 'Givers' and 'Takers'. When you meet someone shake their hand and looked them right in their eyes with a smile on your face, within 15 seconds of doing this you will be able to tell which of the two they are.

The Giver will keep eye contact with you and make a special connection with you. The Taker is the one that will avoid the eye contact but check you out physically. If you are a woman they check you out for your attractiveness because most likely they want something from you, for a man it's generally of a sexual nature. If you are a man they will check out the way you are dressed the way you carry yourself because they are looking for a way to get something from you because most are insecure assholes.

Nana would go on to say always know and feel that you are "Special" as we all are in our own individual way as humans. Secondly when we are comfortable in our own skin which comes with time. Never allow another person to make you feel less about yourself than what you know to be the truth about yourself deep down in your soul. Never give anyone that power over you.

The young boy she used to talk about to me turned out to be her cousin from Cork Ireland, His name was "Michael Collins" he was known as "The Man Who Made Ireland" in the early 1900's. Collins led Ireland to their victory for freedom against England that had ruled Ireland for 700 years in the form of a slave state.

Michael Collins led the fight and victory for Independence in 1921 as a Revolutionary leader of Sinn Fein also known as The Irish Republican Army. He was elected the First President of the First Free Irish Republic. He did great things for Ireland before he was Assassinated on August 22,1922 at the age of 31.

Nana shared these tales with just me over the years just calling him the boy like you. I would find about the rest of the story in 1968 when someone attempted to kill me for the first time.

These were the building blocks that formed my foundation of the man that I have become over these 64 years. A life that I have tried to live with the motto that being a Giver in life and helping others, it is so much more rewarding and carries incredible power in your life to do the right thing
for others.

Preface

November 7,1960, was a monumental day in my life. For on this day my Dad took me to hear a speech by then candidate for the United States Presidency John F Kennedy at Providence City Hall. This was his final campaign rally before being elected the 35th President of the United States on November 8,1960, which happened to be my 8th birthday the next day. I remember feeling it was a great birthday present to me because he was my hero, after reading the book PT 109. Which he saved several of his men from drowning when their boat was cut in half by a large Japanese boat in the Pacific during World War II.

JFK being the First Catholic Elected President was a big deal. This made it that even more special for all of us students at St. Patrick's Middle School in Providence. They brought us downtown to City Hall, where several of my classmates and I were brought up on the stage to meet JFK, shake his hand and stand there while he gave his speech.

I remember these words he spoke that day. He said to the whole crowd that "You can accomplish anything you want to in United States Just Follow Your Dreams. Look at me I am following my dream and I am on the verge of being elected President of the United States tomorrow. Use your Imagination and Always Follow Your Dreams to help guide you through your life." As I have become an adult, those words have stuck with me and I hear them in my head constantly. I go along on this journey to tell the story of my amazing blessed life and all the famous and notorious people that have had positive influences in my life.

I learned as a teen that my family came from Irish Royalty of sorts, because we were descendants of Michael Collins the great fighter and leader of Ireland Revolution in the early 1900s which gave them Independence from Great Britain in 1922. So, we came from a clan of rebels.

I grew up in a world where politics and violence was a very important aspect of your everyday survival. Life in a major city in the northeast like Providence was based on "Who You Were", "Who You Knew", and "Who

You Were With". This really sucked for most of the honest people who felt they never could get a shot at success and security for their family, unless they knew someone who had political power, as my family did.

After meeting JFK and following my Dad around where everyone treated him like he was a big shot and with great respect, or fear as I would learn as I got older was cool. From first time Dad took me into local bar called "The Dew Drop Inn" near the Rhode Island State House were all the important politicians hung out, drank and worked out all their backroom deals.

Well the first time I went in with Dad everyone called out his name "Bull". Give him a beer, give him whatever he is drinking. Like on Cheers TV show years later when Norm would walk in they would yell "Norm". They would sit me in the back booth and feed me meatball sandwiches and cokes to shut me up. I still remember those sandwiches as the best ones I ever tasted.

Dad would sit at the big booth in the corner and do his business, guys would come over to him one at a time and give him money, paper slips, and envelopes full of money and he would put all this stuff in a leather pouch. Other times he would be the one giving out money to the guys. I would just sit there staring at Dad and eating my meatball sandwich making a mess a mess of myself.

It never failed Dad would take out his clean handkerchief and on one corner stick it into his mouth to wet it and then proceed to clean my face with it. I used to yelp come on Dad I can taste your spit. He must have wiped my face with his spit thousands of times in my life and as I sit here now wish he was here to do it one more time.

We would get up and go to the next stop The American Legion and repeat the process. Dad lived in New York during the week while Nana raised us on day to day basis after Mom took off when I was five. My time on Saturday with Dad was like going to Disney World for me.

The home I grew up in was 200 yards away from Rhode Island's State Capital Building. Which is the second largest domed building in the world. All the state and city politicians and mob wise guys knew me, were fond of me because I was John's kid. That can become a crazy and powerful environment to grow up in being treated differently caused lots of issues with other children. I was an angry kid with ADHD, mad about my family life so I beat the shit out of every kid that gave me any shit. It worked for my Dad so why not me I guess I figured.

One of my driving reasons in writing this novel is speak about the many men and women from all walks of life, that had positive influences on my life. Some of these men will be looked on by history as some of the scariest and notorious men in organized crime and politics in the history of America. I knew a different side to these individuals they were part of my family, they were considered my uncles and all wanted the best for me, and always preached to not be like them.

From my perspective, they were businessmen and all had good advice for me and wanted me to do something better with my life, not follow in my Dad's or their footsteps into a life of crime because they all knew there was no long-term future in it.

I also am writing this novel for the Kennedy's because I want to be their voice from the grave and tell American citizens what really happened in the 60's, because we all have the right to know what occurred to JFK and RFK from the mafia's perspective. And to finally put to rest the Disappearance of Jimmy Hoffa in 1975, for the sake of his family.

These stories were told to me by people very close to the situations from the "Organized Crime Perspective" and participated in these "Conspiracies". Ever since November 22,1963, most events that have occurred in the 20th Century have been related to the November 22,1963 event and coverup of JFK'S Assassination.

It is not my intention to try and explain and blame the hundreds of people that were aware in advance and planned the Coup d'etat. It is my intention to tell the American people the truth that it was a Conspiracy plain and simple. The Assassination was set up in three other cities beside Dallas, starting on November 2, in Chicago, November 19, in Miami...Nov 20, in Tampa. The lone gunman shit goes right out the window. The United States Government at the highest levels, CIA, FBI, Mafia, Bankers and four future Presidents of the United States were aware before the fact and part of the greatest cover up in World History.

Some will believe me and some will not. But I feel this my obligation to JFK and to the Americans that grew up in my generation that are entitled to know the truth as I was told from a very different perspective. The Mafia's version of events and the clean-up squads that the Mob and the Cia continued for over 20 years to keep the secret of November 22,1963 a secret. I was told these stories for a reason by my Dad, Frank, Russell, and Raymond Sr in 1978, in Watch Hill RI at the beach house the last time they were ever in each other's company. They all said kid after we are all gone, tell our story to the world if you choose to. You are a smart kid you will figure it out.

For the last 35 years these stories and the recurring dream of JFK telling me to follow my dreams. In speaking to many people about the events in my life and how I survive all the crazy shit I did and experienced and all the famous people I met in my life. I needed to put it on paper. This is my story and my attempt to follow my dreams.

In the Beginning

When we are born, we do not have the choice of who will be our parents or what your family heritage will be or where they come from.

My Grandmother gave me a good solid foundation to help me succeed in life. I came from a family of very strong Independent men, who were not afraid to fight or die for what they believed in.

Michael Collins the leader of Irish fight for independence from Great Britain in the early 1920s. Collins was later elected the First Prime Minister of a Free Ireland. I am proud of the family I was born into.

My birth name is John Francis Sullivan Jr. I was born in Providence, RI on November 8, 1952. Our Family surname is Collins, my family came to America in the 1930s to get away from the political problems in Ireland. Ireland was fighting for independence from the United Kingdom. Civil unrest that took place as independence was won from England. This was led by Michael Collins and a group of 12 young fellas called The Unit. The Unit was a Hit Squad of Assassins that would kill a British Secret Police Detective each time an Irishman was killed.

Michael Collins was a first cousin to my grandmother and uncle Bill. Michael Collins was killed in 1929 at the age of 31. Half of the Collins clan was forced to leave Ireland and come to America and they lived under a different name of Sullivan because of the civil unrest in Northern Ireland that continued for 60 more years between the IRA and Britain.

My story is about survival and vindication, for me and others who had suffered similar problems. To be totally honest about myself and the fact that I survived many addictions, such as alcoholism, drug addiction, sexual, physical abuse, and everything else that's covered under "Addictive Personality". I was sexually and physically abused when I was young by a catholic priest. With the grace of God, I survived and helped by many people as told in this story from all walks in life.

In 1957, my sister and I went to live with our grandmother when our parents divorced. I was five and Margie was seven when our mother dropped us off in front of our grandmother's home at 29 Jewett Street.

She left us with a brown paper bag of clothes and literally drove off. I can still see that moment as if I had a tape recorded in my head. I asked my sister, "What do we do now? She replied, we have to go upstairs to Nana's house."

I had not spent much time there before that. My father was granted custody of us and for a man to get custody in the 1950's was unheard of especially for someone with my father's reputation. Years later I learned that my father didn't have a permanent home for us to live in, which I guess is why we moved in with Nana.

My family had power and very important friends. My father's divorce attorney Joseph Nugent, later became the Governor. My mother Marge Bailey was from Bridgeport, CT. She was a beautiful woman, former Miss Connecticut, blonde, high cheek-bones and was pursued by every guy that spotted her.

She came to Providence to work at Providence College when she met my father. They married and I recall the nonstop fighting from the time I was three. She realized what type of family she had married into and it scared the hell out of her. She gave up custody of me and my sister because she basically feared for her life.

Mom started a relationship with a pilot from American Airlines and was off to travel the world. I would get postcards from all over the world. China, London, etc. it would set my mind into overdrive and imagine what it was like there wherever the card had come from. At a very young age I told myself I was going to get a job with American Airlines someday because being young I thought it was the career of her new husband and that was the reason she left me behind. Of course, it was not, as I would later learn that I came from a family with a lot of secrets and some scary men like my father, my uncles and associates. They were not scary to me because right from the start I was treated very special and different than my sister and 15 or so cousins by my grandmother. The nuns hated me at the schools because they in turn became my full-time babysitters. My sister would take me to where the nuns lived before school started and I would stay there until they left for school and they would escort me to school.

I was a hyper and angry child and was treated much different than the other hundreds of children I went to school with. Of course, kids would think they could pick on the kid that was treated different for some reason and that caused me to lash out and fight every male that crossed my path. I started fighting when I was in 2nd grade. I didn't care who they were or what grade they were in; 7th or 8th graders, in other words, anyone that was a bully at the school.

The nuns called the Providence police when I was in 2nd grade to try and scare me. They took me down to the police station and locked me inside a cell. They told me, "This is what is going to happen to you if you continue to cause trouble and fight again." They thought it was going to scare the piss out of me, well my response was this is better than going to the nuns house every day and night.

I spent a lot of time alone with my little super ball that I always had with me and being left handed I could bounce it with both hands like a pro and it drove everyone nuts. The nuns would yell, "Put that ball away." I would then start tapping my right foot until they would scream stop. I would pick up the ball and bounce it again until it drove them to where they would call me the devil's child, I could not sit still. Being a hyper kid now known as attention deficit hyperactivity disorder or ADHD, I was punished every day of my childhood for doing something and told to go to bed until your father gets home for dinner. While in my room I taught myself how to read and began reading everything in sight. I had to keep myself busy. My father would come and have dinner every night he was in Providence and would then leave. He either goes home to his apartment nearby or out of town to do what we call "Taking Care of Business".

I never lived with either parent again after age five. I never had to take a school book home because I memorized things by looking at them. I would always answer every question in class first and this drove the nuns nuts and crazy. They would say, "Can you let someone else answer a question?"

I was seated in the first seat right in front of every teacher and they were just pawns in my crazy childhood. I do not know why I was so smart. Someone said to me once, "Did you swallow a set of encyclopedias" I replied, "I don't know."

Being raised by my Grandmother, instead of my parents was a blessing in disguise. For one, my mother couldn't handle me plus she had another child from her 2nd marriage. Nana was very strict and protective. She would talk to me about stuff I didn't understand.

This usually occurred while we were watching TV shows, Gun smoke, Rawhide, The Virginian, I Love Lucy to name a few. She had to punished me every day because she didn't know what else to do with me.

I was bad back then and my mouth would always get me in trouble. I didn't do mean stuff, I would say what was on my mind and offend people, like little old ladies with blue hair. I would ask them, "Why is your hair blue?" They would go right to Nana because they were friends with her and tell on me. I would do stuff like that all the time and get busted by the little ole ladies every time.

One could say I was an accident waiting to happen. I got hit by a car one day on my way to the store and another time I fell on a wrought iron fence and it almost killed me. But I'm still here so I guess the Man upstairs has other plans for me.

I was with my cousin and two brothers when one of the boys fell into the Providence River and got stuck in the muck like quicksand and began to sink below the surface. I ran up the road to get help but it was too late. The second brother had jumped in to help his brother to no avail and got stuck himself. I witnessed the second boy going under screaming as he was sucked under. The two brothers who were black drowned right there in a matter of 2 minutes. I felt horrible and helpless and besides I didn't know how to swim. Looking back on it the Man upstairs was protecting me, because if I had jumped in, I would have been lost also.

When I went home I told my grandmother what happened and what I witnessed. She first wanted to kill me for being there when I was not supposed to be, but when I told her about the look on the older brother's face right before he lost his life she stated. "You were supposed to see that and now I have to use this experience in my life". She said that nothing in life happens by chance and she believed our lives are prewritten in the Big Book of Life and it is up to us to keep searching for our destiny. She asked me a short time later if I was afraid of death now and I said no. She said that is why you witnessed what you did and God gave you the gift so few have been given: the gift to live a life of being fearless of the thing all humans fear the most-death. This occurred in August 1960 when I was 8 years old and was the first of many discussions we had about life.

I had a very large extended family, My Grandmother had outlived two husbands. She had seven children which produced 28 grandchildren, most of which she helped to raise. My father was the only boy and therefore her favorite.

When I was brought to live with her at age five when my parents divorced I was considered her baby and favorite of the 28 grandkids. I was also the one who gave her the most problems, being hyper, having ADHD and anger issues about my parents' divorce made me quite a handful to deal with daily for a woman who was 70 years old when I came to live with her.

My sister Margie also lived in the house on 29 Jewett St along with my Great Uncle Bill, my Aunt Marie, her daughter Janet, plus Nana. It was quite crowded in a four-room tenement.

Soon my Uncle Bill passed away and he was the first person I witnessed dying. My sister and I were brought into his bedroom to say our farewell to him. My Uncle Bill had fought with the IRA in Ireland in the 1920's and 30's against England in the fight for Independence for A Free Irish Republic. My extended family included Hagen's, Corry's, McGinn's, Randell's, Sousa's and Bannon's. Nana was the "Matriarch" of our very large clan. We always lived on Smith Hill section of Providence which was in the shadow of the State Capital which was the second largest domed building in the world. Smith Hill was the Irish side of town and a working-class neighborhood with Bars on every street corner.

Nana and my Dad were very powerful people in the neighborhood, so there were always many people around my house on Jewett St asking Nana about certain issues that affect their everyday life: Where they could find jobs and who to go talk to: getting assistance from the State or City to help pay their bills or get food assistance.

My Dad on the other hand was looked on as the toughest guy on Smith Hill, "The Bull" as he was known, was the most feared and respected guy on the Hill. He was known as the guy to go see if you needed to have something done. He took pride in never telling anyone, not when it came to helping anyone out of a jam. His favorite saying was "I took care of that thing for you".

Billy and Bobby Corry were my closest cousins and were always around Nana's house along with Eddie Bannon. Bobby was the oldest four years older than me the youngest of this crew that always seemed to be together, and it was these three that would egg me on to do something crazy that would end up with me being punished every single day of my childhood it seemed. I spent more time in my bed than any other place in my whole life. Go to bed and wait for your Father to get home, which was dinner time each day he was in town.

Also, living in our small home was my Aunt Marie and her Daughter Janet and my sister Marge. Living in such close quarters and me being hyper and always talking and bouncing off the wall drove everyone nuts.

So, all I ever heard was negative thing after negative thing every day from everyone except my grandmother.

She would often tell me how special I was and how gifted I was in many things I did compared to all my cousins. She did not know what to do with me besides send me to my room, which I shared with her and Marge to read or listen to my little radio to the Red Sox game. Even that would drive her nuts at times as I would stay up very late when the Sox were playing on the west coast three hours behind us on the east coast. I only required a few hours' sleep and was up at crack of dawn like the energizer bunny, full of piss and vinegar as my Dad would often say.

My early memories with my Mom before I went to live with Nana were not good ones. For some reason, I was always with my Mom and Marge was with my Dad or at Nana's. I remember numerous car rides between Providence and Bridgeport Ct, where my mother's family lived. Each time I would get car sick, this was the time before seat belts, and I would fly all over the back seat which each turn.

My Mom was a beautiful woman and had many men in her life while separated from my Dad. Going through the divorce and when she would have them over our apartment, I would interfere in all the adult stuff that was going on by not going to sleep. Many times, I made her friends leave early. She would go nuts and beat me; chase me with sticks, brooms, and anything she could get her hands on. I remember one afternoon jumping out a second story window in the projects to get away from her. I was like Superman I did not get hurt.

My worst early memory with Mom was my first day of school at St Anne's in the first grade. Well Mom must have been in a hurry or something that day because she just dropped me off at the curb and I walked into school yard and was told to stand in a line for first graders. I did not know anyone there. My sister Marge was attending another school on the other side of the city. I was standing in line when I had an accident; I had shit myself while waiting in line because of being nervous I guess.

Well the nuns had to take me inside and clean me up and put a raggy old pair of pants on me that made me look bad. So of course, the other kids started making fun of me and as I say the shit hit the fan, because I was not afraid to punch someone in the face that was cracking on me, this day I punched or kicked three other students and had nothing but trouble and was then held back in the first grade. Soon I found myself in St Patrick's Catholic School to repeat the first grade.

My trouble did not stop there. I was not allowed out before school in the school yard, or at recess, or lunch to play with other students. My sister would drop me off at the nuns' house to be walked to school by the nuns. I was a very angry young man because of my mother leaving me on a curb at age of five. The only way I knew how to deal with things was to punch someone or kick them right in the balls and then punch them.

The school called the Providence Police when I was in second grade and they drove me to the Police

Station trying to scare me by showing me a jail cell and locking me inside one. I remember laughing at them and said, "this is better than the nuns house at least there is stuff to see here". Then a cop came in and told the others that I was Bull Sullivan's kid…. So, forget about it. It may be a lost cause. I then said I wanted a lawyer. My Father had always told me first thing to say to a cop is I want my lawyer.

The cops got a good laugh on that one. My first involvement with cops was second grade family record I was told. My fighting and anger issues followed me all the way till 6th grade when I discovered sports to burn off all my anger and energy at St Patrick's Middle School. The fighting has never stopped but we did win four straight City and State Championships in Basketball in CYO youth sports. As it turned out St Pat's was the only school I would ever graduate from in the 9TH grade.

Tim Pat Coogan wrote a book about Michael Collins called, “The Man Who Made Ireland”. The story is based on Michael’s childhood and how special he was treated before his teens. There was a huge age difference between Michael’s mother and father when Michael was 6 years old his father became ill and passed away at the age of 60. His father, on his deathbed told his grieving family to mind Michael because one day he’ll be a great man and do great work for Ireland.

Similar statements were made to me years later by my grandmother. When my grandmother was living out her last hours in a nursing home in 1971, she made my brother-in-law Tony Bucci make a promise to look after me because as she said.” he was very tough to handle but is going to accomplish something great someday.”

Tony promised her he would take me in to live with him and either break my legs or raise me to be a good man. Tony’s family was deeply involved in the Italian Mafia New England Family ran by Raymond Patriarca, who ran the mob from the 1940s till his death in 1984. Patriarca was Joseph Kennedy’s arch enemy and one of the greatest reasons that Robert and John Kennedy pursued the mob and the influence of mob on unions in late 1950s.

Raymond was like a grandfather to me once I met him years later; telling me he loved every Irishman but the Kennedy’s when he found out who my father was he stated, “I know your dad. He works for me from time to time. I always wondered why my grandmother treated and protected me so different than other 15 cousins in my family or even my sister, now I know! My grandmother had seven children, six girls and one boy, John Francis Sullivan, Sr. My Father.

Dad's Early Work

John Francis Sullivan, Sr. aka John Francis was born in Providence RI in 1922. He was a Navy Vet of WW2 when he lied and signed up for the Navy at age of 17, served two years in the pacific on a PT Boat and was involved in some of the worst fighting against the Japs when they went from one island to next, chasing and killing Japs and freeing the US soldiers that were held in prison camps. He returned after the war a changed man.

Soon he found himself involved with a Jewish Gangster named Meyer Lansky who was called "The Brain" because he combined and his mixed bag of Jewish, Italian and Irish mobsters. Dad also had connections with the Irish Republican Army and their fight for Independence from Britain in Northern Ireland.

Meyer saw in my father a very bright young man and a real multi-tasker who meticulously planned and prepared for the jobs he was giving at any given time. Dad was a Fixer/ Cleaner for lack of a better word. After all the early work, Meyer gave Dad, major hits on Mafia Godfather's or Capo's in NYC Family's. My Dad would do similar jobs for Russell Bufalino, Raymond Patriarca, Angelo Bruno, Jimmy Hoffa, Gambino Family, Genovese Family, and The Irish Westies.

My father would always take me to this bar called The Dew Drop Inn. Sit me in the back feeding me meatball sandwiches, one after another, while he would meet with guys at another booth. He was either well respected or feared. As soon as we would walk in, there would be a cheer of "Here's the Bull, give him what he's drinking!" To me they'd say," here's Cement Head", my first nickname because I had cracked my head on the cement sidewalks a few times and never really got hurt. Except once when my sister pulled the pillow back when I was jumping off the bed in the middle of Hurricane Carol 1954, in which I received 18 stitches on right side of forehead which is still there, I remember my Dad saying that was my first passage into manhood many years later. I was three at the time.

It was stuff like that, that scared the hell out of my mother and made her take off in fear. Nana told me at some point that you needed to keep life simple and you'd be alright. She says there are only two kinds of people on earth, Givers and Takers. When you meet someone shake his hand and look him right in the eyes, and within 10 seconds you will be able to tell which one they are. If they can't look you in the eye they are a taker. A taker is a person who is using you or taking something from you. If it's a woman the taker wants to bed the woman. They are greedy and need to take another person's power to survive themselves.

From the first meeting on you own that person because you always know they want something for themselves, she said always be aware of their type but keep them at arm's length away from you, if not out of your life completely. The other type is a giver, like I was raised to be. This is someone who cares for you or anyone else until they are burned or hurt by another in a selfish way.

On April 19, 1951 Vincent "The Executioner", head of the Gambino Crime Family, and his brother Phil, a Capo in the family, disappeared. Their bodies were found in Sheepshead Bay in Brooklyn with several bullets in their heads. My Dad played the role of driver on this hit on the orders of Meyer Lansky and Albert Anastasia who then took over the Gambino Crime Family, after this event. Meyer had great confidence in Dad's ability to plan and facilitate these major operations of knocking off Mob family leaders, with the greatest of discretion as to not start a mob war in NYC.

On October 4, 1951 Willie Moretti was lunching with four other men at Joe's Elbow Room restaurant in Cliffside Park, New Jersey. This is the same Willie Moretti, who 10 years earlier had stuck a gun in the mouth of the Big Band leader Tommy Dorsey, who refused to release Frank Sinatra from his existing contract. Moretti jammed a gun barrel down Dorsey's throat and threatened to kill Dorsey if he did not release Sinatra. Dorsey eventually sold the contract to Sinatra for $1.

The waitress remembered three men, the only patrons in the restaurant, joking together in Italian before she went into the kitchen at 11:28 am. A short stocky man in a dark suit walked in and fired two shots into Moretti, one shot to the face and one to the head. The restaurant staff heard shots fired and ran into the dining room. Moretti was lying dead on his back. By some accounts the shots to the face were a sign of respect, the lone stocky gunman had already fled the restaurant.

This was the first hit my father discussed with me many years later, on the orders of Meyer Lansky. It was also learned later that Jerry Lewis and Dean Martin were supposed to join Moretti for lunch but were warned off by Lansky to not show up.

On the morning of October 25, 1957, three men drove to the Park Sheraton Hotel on fancy Park Avenue in midtown Manhattan. The three men were Joseph "Crazy Joe" Gallo, John "Jackie" Nazarian, and my father who was the driver of the auto. The auto pulled up in front of the hotel near the entrance to the barber shop, when Gallo and Nazarian got out of the auto with their faces covered with scarves and guns drawn and entered the barber shop.

Inside the barber shop was Albert Anastasia, who was head of the "Gambino" crime family, and "Murders Inc" which was responsible for hundreds of unsolved murders. Gallo and Nazarian ran inside the very large barber shop as Anastasia relaxed in the barber chair when they shoved the barber out of the way and fired at Anastasia as he sat there with towels covering his face.

Anastasia then stood up and lunged at the two shooters, the shooters unloaded their handguns into Albert Anastasia and he finally fell to the floor. The two gunmen returned to the auto, where my father was waiting with a handgun in his hand in the event of trouble, and they drove off to switch autos near the airport.

The story made front page news all over the world at the time because of the photos that were published of Anastasia lying on the barbershop floor with blood stained towels. The hit was ordered by the leaders of the Genovese family, Gambino Family, and the Patriarca Family in Providence.

The Appalachian Conference in 1958 was a Mafia summit at a ranch house in rural Appalachian, New York. Russell Bufalino helped organize the meeting for his boss Joseph Barbara, then head of Northeastern Pennsylvania Crime Family. Russell was communicating with delegates, ordering the food and Italian delicacies, and making hotel accommodations for the guests.

On November 15, 101 top American Mobsters gathered, representing all 27 US crime families, along with reps from Canada and Sicily. Attendees included New York family bosses Vito Genovese, Carlo Gambino, Joseph Bonanno, Sam Giancana, of Chicago, Raymond Patriarca of New England, and Santo Trafficante Jr. However, the meeting soon ended in disaster, because

NY State Troopers noticed the reservations being made at local hotels were for mobsters.

Soon Federal and State Agents had surrounded the property and set up roadblocks. Alerted by a deliveryman, the mobsters began to flee. Some ran into the woods while others nonchalantly tried to just drive away, Dad and Russell were arrested along with 69 other well-known mobsters that day. However as with most arrested all charges were eventually dropped. The Appalachian fiasco was a huge blow to the secrecy of organized crime in America. It also took a tremendous toll on Barbara's reputation in the underworld. The humiliation combined with increased law enforcement and media scrutiny, convinced Barbara to retire in 1958.

By the end of the year Russell Bufalino became the de facto boss of the Northeastern PA Crime family. With Barbara's death in June of 1959, The Mafia Commission made Russell Bufalino the official family boss. My Dad served as Bodyguard and Driver for Russell for several years.

Bufalino soon became the epitome of the well-respected, low key, cunning and rational mob boss who knew how to delegate authority and disguise his true power and influence. He was well liked and never flaunted his wealth and power.

In 1963, A low level member of New York Genovese Crime Family, Joe Valachi, testified on the inner workings of La Cosa Nostra to the Senate Select Committee on ties between Organized Crime and the Teamsters Union.

Millions of Americans watched the hearings on television as Valachi named the top Mafia bosses in the US, including Bufalino. The Committee later described Russell as one of the most ruthless and powerful leaders of the Mafia in the United States. Many years later Dad and Russell spent several days on the set of 'The Godfather' as it was being shot in NYC.

By the 1970s Bufalino had become a Senior Mafioso within La Cosa Nostra. It was alleged that in the early 1970s Russell was appointed as the 'Interim Boss' of the Genovese Crime Family by the Commission.

The Westies was another gang my Father was involved in during the 60s and 70s. The Westies were an Irish American gang that operated from Hell's Kitchen on Manhattan's West Side. Although never more than Twenty Members depending on who was in or out of jail at any given time.

The Westies became known as the last generation of Irish in the birthplace of the Irish Mob... According to Crime stats from FBI and NYPD The Westies were responsible for 60-100 murders between 1968 and 1986. My father found himself in tough situations at times because of the Great Irish/ Italian war of the 1970s. Having friends and family on the Irish side with the Westies, and being connected big time with Russell Bufalino and the Genovese Crime family, he found himself in the middle at times and tried to act as a peacemaker.

It was a stupid war over construction jobs and service work at the Madison Square Garden, and later at the Javits Convention Center.

The leaders of the Westies were Mickey Spillane, James Coonan, and Mickey Featherstone until the early 90s.

My Dad told the story about several of the Westies telling him they had the best job in the world. Italian wise guys were paying them to kill Italians, so they could earn their wings to become made men in the Mafia, because they did not have the balls to do it themselves. They loved the fact that Italians were paying them for something they loved to do for nothing.

In 1977 Spillane was assassinated in a hail of bullets by Genovese Hit Men. Then the Bufalino Crime Family, in which Dad was a close associate of the boss Russell Bufalino, Dad eliminated three of Spillane's supporters in Hell's Kitchen. This allowed James Coonan to form an alliance with the Italian Mob, effectively ending the war. Coonan and Featherstone stood trial for Spillane's murder but were found not guilty. A friend of my Dad's Roy DeMao was the killer of Spillane.

The Westies and The Italians worked well together until the 1980s, when a RICO charge came down against Coonan and Featherstone and other Westies for criminal activities going back 20yrs. Featherstone testified in open court for weeks in the trial that began in September 87 and concluded with major convictions in 1988.

Coonan was sentenced to 60 years. The remaining Westies were sentenced to 40 years on loan sharking and drug related charges. At this point in time, the Russians and the Serbs took control of Hell's Kitchen and all the Rackets.... My Dad had a saying "The Only Good Russian is a Dead One"

My Meeting JFK

On November 7, 1960, Providence was all a buzz as John F. Kennedy was holding his last rally at the Providence City Hall before Election Day, the eve of JFK being elected the first Irish Catholic President of the United States.

I was on the stage with a bunch of other kids from St. Patrick's Catholic School, which was right across from city hall. JFK was shaking everyone's hands when he came up to me and I said to him, "You are my hero" He said, "Why is that" I said, because of PT 109, you saved your men from drowning. I know how hard that is because earlier this summer I was with two friends that had drowned right in front of me and I could not save them". He then said to me, "God bless you son, you are too young to see that, I know how hard that must have been".

Years later after the death of JFK, I remembered him saying, "You can become anything in this country that you can dream of, just always follow your dreams". I remember him grinning ear to ear and saying something like, "This guy is a live one and not shy to talk, huh". I still can hear those words today in my head. He also was elected the following day on my 8th birthday - November 8th, 1960, the first Irish Catholic President, which in my mind reinforcing my connection to him. Nothing in Life Happens by chance, my grandmother used to say.

JFK had a real influence in a lot of events that went forward in my life and the people that I met and was related to. Some of the influential people were very notorious and important figures in the 19th century, such as my Dad John Francis, Frank Sheeran, Raymond Patriarca, Meyer Lansky, Nicky Bianco, Gerry T, Kevin Hanrahan, Jimmy Hoffa, Tony Bucci, Russell Boyle, Billy Corry, Sal Bellavia, and Russell Bufalino. All of which were classified as Italian Godfathers or enforcers or influential politicians. They all had positive influence in my life. In my opinion, they were" Good Stand Up Guys".

My First Home Run

In 1963, I was about 11 years we had just gotten a color TV, first in the neighborhood. Nana kept a wooden baseball bat up against the wall next to the window in the bedroom that she and I shared. We lived on the first floor and I asked her why the bat was there. She said it was there for us to use on someone for breaking in the house to rob us or hurt us. She said, if needed, just grab it and crack them right the in head before they get in here.

Sometime later we were awakened by someone opening the window in the middle of the night, she said softly, "Jonny get the bat", I did and waited for the guy to put his head in the window and I cracked him as hard as I could, the guy ran away screaming and left blood all over the window sill. She said, "Good boy", and patted me on the head.

Later my father shows up, fit to be tied, and leaves quickly. He comes back several hours later dressed in different clothes, smiling. He pats me on the head saying, "Great Job! Don't worry that will never happen again, I took care of it. There were two of them involved, you will never see them again". Then says, "Mom I took care of our little problem". She says I knew you would".

We never discussed it again and never had any more problems ever again. I do not know what my dad did but can only imagine! They paid a heavy price for breaking into the wrong place.

My father remarried when I was 10-12, but I did not go live with him, I stayed with my grandmother. I was an angry child because until 6th grade I was not allowed to play in the school yard before school recess, lunch or after school. I was never and I mean never allowed to play or fight with other students till the age of 12-13, or so.

That only changed when I discovered basketball and other sports. It did not take me long to use my hyper energy ADHD before they knew what it was. All my life I have had a resting heart rate of 130-140, which is almost twice the rate of normal people or kids.

In the next 4 or 5 years, I became one of best basketball players and athletes in the northeast. In Providence in the 1960s and 70s, it was like the mecca in the world of basketball. The Boston Celtics practiced in gyms and outside courts in my area. They ran camps that I attended for free for weeks at a time. They sent us to camps at Duke University in NC for free. In the next 5 or 6 years, we won 5 state, city and New England championships, almost being undefeated each year.

We were always around famous coaches and players, like Bill Russell, Red Auerbach, Bob Cousy, coach Joe Mullaney of the LA Lakers. We were on first name basis with our idols. All the rules were broken for me in school as an athlete. I was offered scholarships to seven different high schools for four different sports. Because I could run a 10.2 second 100-yard dash, and dunk a basketball. This was due to the energy from having one or two extra gears from my heart rate.

I chose a school named Mt Pleasant, the coach had played professional ball with the Celtics years before. As a 9th grader, not even in high school yet, they allowed me to play at away games to get experience. I was already the best player on team. I did not have to really study in school because they always passed me to play ball. Next year, I was the first 10th grader to start in the "A" division in school history, and earned a third team Allstate Honor. I also earned letters in track and football as a 10th grader.

This all came to a screeching halt in August 1968 when the attempt on my life occurred. I was 16 years old. I already had a summer job working overnight for US Post Office unloading trucks and trains of mail. A local Irish Politician named Russell Boyle, who was most powerful politician in Providence, just gave me and three other friends part time jobs to earn money, and stay in great shape. We would work two hours get paid for eight. Russell Boyle game about 12 other jobs over the years including as his bodyguard at times when he had a few to many at some political events. I know the healthy respect he had for my Dad had something to do with it.

maybe it's your turn to get shot. The only way to survive this kind of life is to fight back. If you don't, your time on this earth will be short-lived.

Ambulances came and transferred the mortally wounded and other injured boys to the hospital. I was taken to the police station for questioning. I couldn't tell them anything or ID the shooter as I was in shock. My dad showed up with his lawyer. He threw me over his shoulder to his car, never saying a word. He took me home to my Grandmother's house. My grandmother yells at my father, "What happened, are you responsible for this or is it the IRA?" He did not have an answer. She knew my father was in a shady business and never wanted to know what he was doing. The next day I asked my grandmother what was she talking about when she said the IRA, which I had heard of but did not know much of its history.

Finally, she discussed the family history with me. She told me about our family being sought after by the IRA, the Irish Government, and the Brits for acts during the revolution by Michael Collins and by my Uncle Bill for Revenging Michael's Collins assassination.

I discovered that I couldn't go to sleep at night. The only way to rid my mind of that incident was to drink a couple of beers before going to bed. Regrettably, the results were huge for me as I became an alcoholic right from first drink. I never returned to high school on a regular basis or played sports again. I started drinking on a daily -basis while bunking school, and then I just quit school. There was myself and four or five friends that bunked and drank beer a lot, -

approximately five cases a day and you needed money to pay for the beer every day. So, a friend, Bob R. taught us how to raise the money. Bob taught us to steal copper drain pipes that were on the side of every house, we would sell them to Charlie Fink at Douglas Avenue Junkyard. The police determined in the span of seven months, we stole over $20,000 in copper drain pipes. The police arrested Charlie. None of us were ever arrested.

I started hanging out with the wrong people like Irish Mobsters that were involved with my father. My problem was I had a great deal of guilt about the previous year shooting. I knew it was all because of me and my family that my friends had died. I went from an athlete who had the world by the balls, to one who dropped out of school. Even though I never went higher than 10th grade, I managed to pass the GED test on the first day two years later, without practicing or taking study classes. Soon after that I was given my first city job.

At the age of 17, I had my start into the Irish and Italian underworld. I was collecting money for gamblers and hitting the front pages of newspapers, when a friend of mine and myself went into a bar to collect a debt owed to Ronnie Coppola with baseball bats. Eleven guys were injured. Loansharking and numerous other charges were dropped for lack of witnesses.

One Friday night I was out drinking in Fall River, Mass, with a friend we both had too much to drink and the police arrested us. They handcuffed us and were bringing us to the police station. When we arrived at the station I made a run for it handcuffed and all. I ran down the alley and the police fired three shots over my head into a brick wall to get me to stop running.

Dad arrived in court with his lawyer the next morning and was not happy with the situation, I paid a fine and was sent home. It was a very long ride back to Providence in silence. Someone was very angry at me pulling a very stupid stunt.

Dad, Frank & Russell

My Dad was involved with several Italian mob family's, including the Patriarca family, and Bufalino family of New York. He served as a driver for Russell Bufalino and was the partner of Frank Sheeran.

Frank Sheeran and my father were like Mutt and Jeff. Frank was a big man, 6'4" 250 lbs. and my dad 5'8" 200 lbs. They were like the odd couple in many ways; Frank always had a smile on his face and my dad looked like he wanted to bite your face off. Frank was a talker like me and dad didn't say shit, unless he had to.

Frank was in his early 20's in 1941 when he entered the Army. He came home a very different man. He spent over 400 days in combat in Europe during WW2 with Patton's Army, which swept across Italy, France, and into Germany. If Patton had his choice he would have gone through Russia, because he knew we would be at odds with Russia soon after the war. Patton was forced to retire because of this.

Patton did not want German Prisoners of war, it would slow him down. He felt he could not feed them, and had nowhere to house them. The soldiers were told to take them away and kill them behind a house or wall. This occurred hundreds of times, Frank said. He was a changed man when he returned, as was my father on his return from the Navy.

After a year or so, Frank finally got a job driving a truck when he returned home, which is where he met Russell Bufalino one day when his truck broke down. This little old man who happened to be a Mafia Capo, helped fix his truck. They became good friends for the rest of their time alive. Russ dubbed Frank "The Irishman". His new Italian friend solved Frank's aptitude for violence, and his passion for the teamsters' union, to become a valued asset and best buddy to Bufalino and Jimmy Hoffa.

Frank told my Dad that in October 1963, Russell asked Frank to deliver a duffel bag to Baltimore. He handed it over to David Ferrie, a pilot for Carlos Marcello, the New Orleans Mafia Boss who was always thought to be part of the JFK killing.After Kennedy was killed, Frank often wondered if he had supplied the weapons to have him killed. He felt guilty because he was fond of Jack Kennedy, because he was a vet like himself.

My Dad had delivered three Rifles to someone in Chicago around the same time on the orders of Russell. It was later learned that they were to be used at the Assassination Attempt of JFK in Chicago on Nov 2, at the

Army-Navy Game. The attempt never took place because Kennedy was warned by the secret service.

Frank first met my Dad in 1953 in NYC at a Teamster's Convention. They were partners until 1980 when Frank was put in federal prison for extortion. Frank died of old age in a nursing home in 2003. I do not believe they had any contact in the last 20 years. However, Frank and Russell did time together in Danbury Federal Prison in the early 90's. Russell died at home in Scranton in 1998, I believe. Dad died in 2002 in a nursing home in East Providence, RI.

Life on Smith Hill

I spent my first 17 years on Smith Hill on the Irish side of town. At 16, I held my first real job at the US Post Office, where I worked during the summer at night unloading trains. I was making as much money as grown men, showing up when I wanted to and still being paid. I thought I was hot shit and was given just about any job I wanted, until I got sick of it or the boss I had to work for turned into an asshole. In this case, I gave him a piece of my mind by telling him go fuck himself or something worse. I knew where the power laid, my father John Francis and Russell Boyle, a friend of my father's.

Over the next eight years or so, I had three state jobs, four city jobs, and two other part time jobs at the Providence Civic Center, and the Post Office as a 90-day temp. In 1969, I started working for the City of

Providence. Russell Boyle was my Rabbi or Political Connection.

I was paid to go into a bar by a Major Mobster named Ronnie Coppola, who was a big bookie and loan shark, and lent out money with very high interest. Billy Daley a childhood friend, from Smith hill was the toughest kid I knew. Together, we went into a bar with baseball bats to break the owners arm, because he was not paying Ronnie the money he was due.

There was a problem inside the bar, six to eight guys had to get wacked with the bats besides the owner getting a broken arm and a busted head. Someone called the cops and this event made front page news the next day in the Providence Journal. Billy and I were arrested and charged as adults even though we were only 17. A very expensive lawyer showed up to get us out of jail. Charges were dropped because no witnesses would identify Billy or I out of fear.

On February 8, 1970, I was visiting the Pantry, the Pantry was a mob hangout near the state capital. My brother in law Tony was the manager there, it was a front for a group of wise guys including Mob Capo Louie "The Fox" Taglianetti.

This night around 7:30 pm it was starting to get dark. Louie "The Fox" was at the restaurant eating dinner with his girlfriend Liz. They finished their meal, and left out the backdoor of the restaurant. In the parking lot, there was an automobile with two men inside the vehicle with shotguns. They fired several rounds at Taglianetti and his girlfriend, killing them both. Taglianetti was shot in the back of the head and Liz's face was blown off. No one could or would ID the shooters. At the time of Taglianetti's death, he was under indictment for the 1962 murder of Jackie Nazarian, a shooter my Dad had worked with in the past.

This was a time when Providence was being compared to the wild west. There were mob hits going on every week, Gerard Ouimette, known as "The Frenchman" was at war on the southside of Providence with the Greens and the Bacons over the takeover of The Bronx Tap on Broad St. There were assassination attempts on a nightly basis by both sides. The Frenchman finally won out and took control of the south side of Providence.

My Time in the Army

Early in 1970, I was making a mess of my life on the street, and would probably end up in jail or dead if I didn't do something about it. Every year the Army would pull the lottery numbers to see who will be drafted. I was lucky again when my number came out 334, which was high enough that I would not have to worry about the draft. I knew I needed a change, so I started asking around. I spoke to Lou Melise, who was a member of the RI National Guard unit,19th Special Forces at the Cranston Armory. I did all the testing, did very well, extremely high and was told I would be going to boot camp in three weeks at Ft. Dix. From there jump school, then Infantry school and other specialty training in small and large arms.

Being a smart ass and wanting to make sure this is what I really wanted to do, you know, see if I liked it and all before making a commitment of it, almost got me thrown out of the Guard before I even started. The unit was having a jump on a Saturday morning and I was supposed to stay on the sideline and watch the others do their training jump. Well I did not do that, in all the confusion I got a parachute and snuck onto the helicopter. I stood in line and went out the open door, and made my first jump. Well the unit commander went off the wall when he found out about my jump.

Things got hot and heavy that following week. My commander came to me and said the regular Army is offering you $2000 if you re-sign with them and go on active duty for two years. They feel that you have bright future and will give you best training in the 5th Special Forces Airborne. It did not take me long to take their offer. $2000 was a lot of money then, but I did not look at the big picture as I was surely sending myself to Southeast Asia for sure. In less than a week I was sent to Ft. Dix for basic training, then to Ft. Benning for jump school, then to Ft. Bragg to learn to Special Force training.

In May of 1971, I was done with training and was sent to Vietnam. Cambodia and Laos is where Special Ops did most of their work. I was part of a program called the Phoenix program. Which was small platoon groups usually on search and destroy of high value officers to disrupt the traffic along the Ho Chi Minh Trail.

I was in the country when Nixon was caught carpet bombing Laos and Cambodia and thousands lost their lives. I returned home in January of 1972 when they pulled all Special Ops out of Vietnam because of the in fighting with the CIA. I had spent eight months in Asia and given an Honorable Discharge on Jan 20, 1972.

I had just landed back on American soil from Guam back to San Francisco, and all the way I had replayed the 240 days of hell I had just experienced. I could see Anti- War Protesters along the outside fence protesting the return of all returning Vets, holding signs that were saying "Baby Killers", "Murderers" and many other things. San Francisco was the main airport for returning Vets and the main center of protesters to the war in the 60's and 70's.

I did not have to look at the protestors to make me feel shitty. I was already carrying around my own demons of what I did over there. I had heard of Vets returning home and being spat on, and suffering other abuses from protesters. I made up my mind to never allow someone to do any of that crap to me, without knocking them on their ass.

As I reached the tarmac I spotted a dumpster near the entrance to the terminal and I threw my duffel bag into it, because this was my way of trying to move on from all the bad experiences of last two years.

I then went upstairs to the terminal and bought myself some jeans, shoes and a sweatshirt. I went into the men's room to change out of my Army uniform. There was a long-haired dirty hippie standing there staring at me as I walked into the stall to change. I finished quickly to catch my connecting flight back to Providence. Well the hippie was standing in front of the urinal facing me as I exited the stall. He said to me," Are you afraid to wear your uniform, because you are one of those baby killers from Viet Nam". I was shocked but said, "Fuck You Asshole," and hit him with a left jab that broke his nose; blood was coming out heavy. He was still standing yelling something at me, so I threw a quick right that landed on his jaw, the blow put him on the floor near the urinal. Somehow, I pushed his head in the urinal on the floor and flushed it several times as he was crying like a baby. Other people came in then, and I had to leave quickly. I ran to the gate of my next flight that was already boarding, and ran down to the tarmac and up on the aircraft to hide so I would not be arrested.

It was a long 15 minutes before we took off. I was holding my breath the whole time. I felt stupid thinking why did I join the Army in the first place? All of this made me start thinking about what I was returning to back in Providence, where everyone I knew was a wise guy or leg breaker, or like my Dad and Frank-contract Killers for the Mafia. I had seen too many deaths in the last eight months and it was already starting to give me nightmares.

Then there was the letter my birth mother had sent me in Nam, explaining to me that she had not abandoned me and my sister when I was five years old. She claimed she was forced to leave by my Dad and she was afraid he would kill her and her family. At the time, I was born my Dad was working for Meyer Lansky, and he would move all over the place moving Meyer's money around the world as what's called money laundering. He was also a driver, bodyguard, and jack of all trades. He would later work for Russell Bufalino, a Boss for several New York Crews, and the Patriarca family that ran the Mob in New England.

This scared the hell out of my mother, so she ran. I did not blame her for running, but it took me many years to forgive her. The feeling of abandonment at the age of five is not something you get over easy.

My Return to Providence

I walked through the small Providence Terminal Airport and out the front door. The first thing I see is a big Lincoln four door with my Dad and Frank

Sheeran standing in front talking to an airport cop. They both were smoking big Cuban Cigars leaning on the auto like they owned the Airport. Dad spots me and yells out, "It's all or nothing with you huh. No bags with you huh", I said I threw them away.

Dad and Frank both give a big hug, and kisses on both cheeks and say, "Welcome home in one piece and not in a box". Frank roars, "Look who's in the back-seat, Russell came to welcome you also". Russell was my Dad's employer at that time and Acting Godfather of the Genovese Crime Family in NYC. Frank then says we are here to protect you from the protesters or is it that were protecting them from you. We don't want you to kill any protesters here your first day back. Dad says we heard of your little adventure out on West Coast. Russ says trouble seems to find you kid. I jump in back seat with Russell who kisses me on both cheeks and said welcome home. Now to get you a good job right kiddo, I nod yes sir. On my way, back to Nana's house it was decided for me that I would return to my job with the City of Providence.

In 1971, somehow my Father found out who the shooter was at the Pizza World that tried to kill me back in 1968. He would not tell me the shooters name, only that he was from the Boston area and was connected to the Irish Mob up there. "He did tell me that he took care of it".

My Dad had the guy followed and found out he walked his dog every morning at 5:30AM. Early one morning when the guy was walking his dog before day break, My Dad waited in some bushes for the guy to walk by. Then he stepped out of the bushes and confronted the guy. "You knew that I would deal with you someday "right"? The guy said yes and then asked for a favor. He asked my dad if he would return the dog to his house and just put it over the fence. My Dad said yes, "I Love dogs too". My Dad then fired two shots into the guy's head just behind his ear. My Dad then picked up the Dog and put him over the fence. He then waved for his wheelman to pick him up to leave the scene. This hit remains unsolved.

In 1972 when I first met Raymond Patriarca, the head of the Mob in New England, I was now fully aware of who my father was and who his friends were in the business of organized crime on a national level.

My father was also very close to Jimmy Hoffa and the Teamsters Union. He was considered close enough to be a bagman for Hoffa. He was always traveling, which was why I lived with my grandmother until she passed away when I was 18, because I very seldom saw my father in the early years.

Raymond Patriarca was an Italian American mobster from Providence, RI. He was born in Worcester, Massachusetts and was longtime boss of the Patriarca crime family. His control extended throughout New England for over three decades. Patriarca was one of the most powerful crime bosses in the United States. He often served as a mediator between warring crimes families outside the region. He would compile a list of criminal charges during his teenage years for hijacking, armed robbery, assault, safecracking, auto theft, and accessary to murder before prohibition ended in 1934.

Despite being named Public Enemy No. one by the Providence public safety during the 40's he served only several months on a five-year sentence for armed robbery after being released by state officials in 1948. It was later discovered that Patriarca had paid off the Governor of RI. Governor Charles Hurley was later impeached, despite the scandal Patriarca reputation in the underworld was enhanced due to his demonstration of political connections.

Patriarca's reign as leader of the New England syndicate was reportedly a brutal and ruthless one. In the early 1960s Raymond was again caught talking to then Governor John Notti on the first wiretap in US history discussing a $10,000 bribe.

In 1960, he was involved in the hit on Cuban President Fidel Castro by the CIA, which they had paid him 2 million dollars to kill Castro which never came to fruition.

Crazy Joey Gallo

In 1972 friends of mine Donald De Mello and Billy Daley asked me to go to NYC to help move his Godfather Nicky Bianco's furniture back to Barrington, RI, with him and two other guys from the neighborhood. So, I did. Donald and I start fighting over something stupid and Nicky had to break us up. He laughs at me and says, "You remind me of myself. You fight at the drop of hat like I used to."

It took about 12 hours by the time we got back and put furniture the in the new house. Until that day, I had never heard of Nicky Bianco. I later found out he was a very well-known Mobster from Providence who had been sent to NYC years earlier and was part of the Colombo crime family which is one of the five leading families in the US and NYC.

Nicky was also part of a renegade group of mobsters mainly led by gangster Crazy Joey Gallo and his three brothers and a group of black thugs that Joey Gallo had spent time in jail with, and they wanted to bring drugs into NYC against the orders of the five families.

They had one of the black guys attempt to kill Joe Colombo at the Italian American Parade in NYC in early 1972.

Colombo survived a gunshot wound to the head and the shooter was killed on the spot, but it set off a race war in the city and set off a mob war between the five families.

Bianco's association with the Gallo's became a grave problem for him because Bianco was in NYC on the protection of Patriarca, Raymond was ordered to resolve this issue by getting rid of Joey Gallo or else.

A few weeks after the furniture move with my friends from NYC to Rhode Island, I was asked by Nicky to have my Dad contact him for a business matter. I spoke to my Dad and relayed the message to Dad and some plan was put in motion. Well, it all accrued as planned when John Francis and Frank Sheeran showed up to kill Joey Gallo in an Italian restaurant down the street from the Nicky's condo on Mulberry St. I was not aware until next day what it was all about when I read newspapers or seen it on TV, because it was the biggest story for about a week across the country.

After that I became very familiar with Bianco who was in Providence then, and was grateful to me and my father for saving his ass as he would later say.

Another Day God Had My Back

I had been back from Nam about six months and had my share of trouble since returning. My reputation was as a crazy guy, I was approached by a guy named Boy Mao. About being a getaway driver on a bank job up on the east side of Providence. I did not know him well but knew he was trouble and had done time in the past. I said to him no way what are you nuts. I said that's not for me, I don't shoot at cops or get shot at by cops. I knew he was not happy with my answer and he walked away mad.

I forgot all about the conversation. To make a long story short Boy and three other guys went to the bank on the east side, where the police were waiting for them to come out of the bank after robbing it. They blew all four of them away on the sidewalk in front of the bank. For several days, it was big news in Smith Hill.

Several days later, a Friday night, I was hanging at the Polish Club drinking when a brother of one of the guys killed comes in and calls my name out. He has a handgun in his hand and points it at my head. He says you set them guys up to be killed at the bank. I said," are you fucking nuts and you don't have the balls to pull that trigger" And I spit in his face which was not too smart. He turned and walked away.

There were several off-duty cops behind me luckily that night. My Dad found out and chewed my ass out for being a jackass and spitting in the guy's face.

POLITICS PROVIDENCE STYLE

One night in 1973 it was near dusk and I was up on Broadway hanging out at Berarducci Funeral Home. Nicky Bianco pulls in the big driveway and stops. He looked over at me and nods for me to come over to him.

I walked over to his auto and said, "What are you doing here?" He said, "I'm here to see Cianci," meaning Buddy Cianci, the guy running for mayor of Providence.

Well it turns out that Cianci's family owns the large apartment building next to the funeral home on Broadway. Suddenly Buddy Cianci is standing on the other side of the iron fence about 50 feet away. He waves for Nicky to come over and talk.

I stayed at the auto and Nicky goes over to the fence and talks to Buddy for 15 minutes or so. He then returns to the auto, I said "What did that asshole want?" Nicky says, He wants us to get him a few democratic votes so he can win. He said he will give me 10 no show jobs if he wins."

You have any ideas how we can pull this off, I said we can get a bunch of absentee ballot. My sister does that shit all the time. I know the last time she had 22 people vote from her house. Then I told him about Arthur Jones, a guy I knew that work at the auto registry that could get phony Id's. And this would allow people to vote multiple times. I had heard of this system that a black politician in South Providence had used in the past in which he would get a group of people together that he trusted and would get multiple Drivers Licenses for these people to vote in all 13 Wards in the City of Providence.

This system would bring in several hundred extra votes for the politician they were supporting. We came up with a list of people that we trusted both Irish and Italian from the 12th and 13th Wards with very common last names and had fake driver licenses made out in 18 people's names and they proceeded to vote 13 times for Cianci's first election. In a city, the size of Providence, 234 votes are very significant. In the end Cianci won by 708 votes. He came through with the 10 City Jobs.

In January 1973, I started dating my first wife Wendy and before we knew it she was pregnant with my son John. It certainly was not a marriage made in heaven. I was told it was the right thing to do by many men in my life including my Dad, Russell, Raymond, and my brother-in-law Tony. Ai the time I was living with Tony and Margie on Ridge St up on Federal Hill.

Margie was the only one that was against it. She stated that Wendy was using me to get out of her parents' home because she was the rebellious type and she was a nymphomaniac. Everything my sister said was correct and our marriage was really one of convenience, but the problem was she kept getting pregnant. My son John or Jay, which he is known as today was born on February 16,1974 and my daughter Kelly was born February 19, 1976 so before I knew what hit me I was the father of two children.

I was already working two jobs the city job and at the civic center as a security guard and set up guy when needed. I was also an extra in movies that came to RI like "The Way We Were" and "The Great Gatsby" both starring Robert Redford. I was always busy with something trying to make enough money and really missed a great deal of time with my two children while they were growing up. In 1983, my son Matthew was born and I would have questioned him being my son, if he did not look like my twin and just like Jay. Also at the same time, Wendy was cheating and our marriage only lasted seven years.

Billy Dailey

I was out drinking one night at Smith Hill Tap on Smith Street in Providence with several friends including Billy Dailey. We all had too much to drink but especially Billy. At 11 pm or so we left the tap and started bar hopping, going from one bar to the next on foot. The first one we get to was Harry's Tap. This is a bar where a lot of mobsters hang out and play cards and shoot craps. It was late on a Saturday night and there were just a few guys in, there when we arrived.

Big Eddie V was behind the bar when we went in, Eddie was part of the Italian mob that ran the club. Eddie and Billy did not like each other because Eddie was always busting Billy balls about stuttering and thinking he was a tough guy. Billy was a tough guy but Eddie was much bigger, and a bully.

Something is said and it starts a beef between the two, Eddie comes from behind the bar and punches Billy and drives him back to where the table that had the hot dogs laid out for everyone to eat. Well Billy knocks the table over, everything hits the floor including him and a large bread knife. As Billy rises, Eddie is charging at him to hit him again when Billy came up with the knife in his hand, and drives it into Eddie's big fat belly. Eddie is stunned for a second, but still tries to attack Billy, when

Billy stabbed him again right through the heart and Eddie hit the floor screaming and cursing.

I stood there with my mouth wide open in shock. It happened so fast and I was out the door as fast, as I came in. Billy and a guy named Harvey followed me out, but I went in the opposite direction as them. Billy still had the knife in his hand and then threw it down the sewer-hole in front of the bar.

Billy was convicted and ended up doing three years. From what I heard, a lot of shit hit the fan because Eddie was an Italian mobster. I was very lucky not to be charged with conspiracy for being present when the murder occurred. My friend Harvey who was also there was charged with conspiracy. My Dad made some calls and got me out of being at the wrong place at the wrong time.

Buddy's First Term

If it was possible, Buddy Cianci's election to Mayor as the first Italian-American in the history of Providence as an anticorruption candidate of all things, took corruption to a level never seen before in history, with fixing of elections to start, in bed with the mob, payoffs, no show workers, union payoffs and kickbacks to Cianci in the hundreds of thousands. The Irish Democrats previously held the monopoly on this position for 150 years until Cianci was elected.

On January 6, 1975, Buddy Cianci was sworn in as mayor and from day one of his first administration, as the anti-corruption candidate, he was surrounded by everybody that he had made deals with to get elected. They included Larry McGarry the 10th ward boss, Tony Bucci 4th ward boss, Philip "Sharky" Almagno, 7th ward boss, and Lloyd Griffin. Lloyd was a up and coming black political figure who had worked for former Mayor Doorley. As did Ronnie Glantz who was now a top aide to Cianci.

The no show jobs that were promised to Nicky Bianco were fulfilled and most were assigned to Public Works and the Highway Department. But the fighting and back stabbing started soon after Cianci was sworn in. Between the Italians in the 4th ward, and the Italians in the 13th ward of Federal Hill. This was over who would control the purse strings at Public Works where most of the Federal money from grants and taxes would go.

There were numerous clashes between Cianci and the city council and the labor unions. Cianci was known to show up for something as small as a letter opening to draw attention to him. I played for the city of Providence softball team for several years.

In April of 1975, Buddy shows up at our first practice with snowflakes coming down; he jumps out his limo, grabs a bat, starts hitting balls, not too well I must say, then grabs a glove, runs out on the field to shortstop, and is diving like a whack job at all ground balls that comes his way. Then he ran back to his limo and was gone.

Soon afterwards there was a riot at city hall during a city council meeting between city workers, police and the democratic council members about the budget and layoffs.

After this event, the Democratic City Council President Robert Haxton was arrested and charged with trying to sexually assault a young boy who was 16 at the time. Everyone screamed it was a set up to force the City Council to give Cianci the budget he wanted, and it worked. Along with Cianci getting Federal Funds from Washington, the Ford Administration brought in a lot of money to the city.

During Cianci's 1st administration in the 70s and 80s, I was extremely close to some of the biggest players in Cianci's back pocket, which resulted in me having personal knowledge of the corruption scandals that went on during that time. Despite my position and the information, I had, I was only in the company of Buddy Cianci a dozen or so times. I never attended any political get-togethers for the so-called p*oliticians* because I did not kiss anyone's ass, especially crooked politicians and believe me; they all were in Rhode Island.

In 1976 Ronnie Glantz was Buddy's top aide. He said in my presence one day when I was in his office with "Buckles" and Anthony Blackjack that Cianci tolerated corruption because the Mayor was the biggest crook of them all.

Glantz said he was an eyewitness to the corruption at City Hall because he was Buddy's bagman. This was something we were aware of because everything went through Ronnie Glantz. Back in the beginning, when the mob helped Cianci get elected for the first time in 1974, with Nicky Bianco's help, my work with fake id's, Buckles and Blackjacks work in the 13th ward with the machines and absentee ballots helped get Cianci elected. Glantz was always the middle man.

When he was not doing the Mayor's bidding, he had us extorting snowplow contractors, shaking down garbage truck dealers, stealing asphalt, and perfecting the art of the no show jobs, a proud Providence tradition. We were looting city equipment right down to manhole covers, which were sold for scrap metal. Glantz was also trading city contracts for cash and rigging the bids. Most of the contracts went through Public Works and the highway department, where Buckles and Blackjack had complete control of everything.

During my tenure with the Public Works Department, I was promoted to Sidewalk Inspector because I was a very dependable employee, not to mention the fact that I was probably the smartest employee there. That's not a pat on my back but because everyone else in Public Works were not the sharpest bunch of guys. Even the engineers with degrees were half brain dead, or certainly did not have much street sense on how to do stuff and get away with it.

The Public Works administration required everyone to take an IQ test for a state license, I finished at the very top. So, with my brains and street sense I was a very valued employee, plus I could be trusted to never talk about anything and was always assigned the most difficult projects.

Frank's Big Night 1974

Frank Sheeran Appreciation Night was on August 18,1974. My Dad invited me to Frank's night, which he was to be giving a plaque for Teamsters Man of the year, and to talk to Jimmy Hoffa to get him to agree not to pursue the Leadership of the Teamsters Union this year because he was scaring many people in the Mob and President Nixon and John Mitchell and the Cia to name a few.

They closed the Latin Club for the event to honor Frank. Jimmy Hoffa was the keynote speaker, 3000 people attended the event. I was seated at a table up front with my Dad, Russell Bufalino, his wife Gail, Angelo Bruno, Boss, of Philly Mob.

When the event was over after Jerry Vale and the Gold Diggers performed, the hall cleared out. The big meeting took place in a small side room with Dad, Frank, Russell, Angelo Bruno and myself standing guard at the double doors to not allow anyone in. Russell spoke loud and stern to Hoffa, He asked him," why are you running? You don't need the money? "Hoffa replied" I'm not letting Fitz fuck me out of my union". Russell then turned to Hoffa and said, "There are people a lot higher than me that feel that you are demonstrating a failure to show appreciation for 'Dallas' in 63."

Jimmy never responded to Russell, who just looked away and that meant the meeting was over.

Russell then turned to Dad and Frank and said take your friend back to his hotel and talk some sense into him, and get those two bags from him before you leave the hotel.

Back at Jimmy's hotel the Warwick Jimmy was in a rage, everyone wants me to back down, they're all afraid of what I know, now they have Russell leaning on me. I have more records, and don't even think about what you think you know, I have more records that I can send out to the media. I'll bring them all down-Nixon, Mitchell, Santo, Carlo, and that fucking prick Tony Pro. Dad and Frank told Jimmy he was going down the road of no return. Jimmy yells very loud "'They would not dare. Nobody scares "Hoffa". Dad and Frank grabbed the two bags and left, shaking their head, saying this is not going to end well. They both were very fond of Jimmy and had worked with him for many years. The two bags contained Hundreds of Thousands of Dollars. One bag for John Mitchell, and the other for the Russell and the Mob in NYC. Frank tried to get Jimmy to stand down one more time in 1975.

My dad was a member of the Teamsters Union for many years. He and Frank Sheeran were close friend with Teamsters President Jimmy Hoffa, so it was easy for them to get close to Hoffa at a moment's notice. President Nixon had given Hoffa a get out of jail pass with one condition. He could not pursue the Union Presidency until at least 1980. Well it did not take Hoffa long before he started making waves and causing trouble for the Mafia, Nixon and Union leadership.

Hoffa believed he had the trump card over everyone, because it was the Teamster's pension fund that paid for the JFK assassination. Of the $700,000 payment, $350,000 went to Carlos Marcello and Santo Trafficante, the Mob leaders of New Orleans and Tampa, and $350,000 went to Richard Nixon, former Vice President. The money went to Nixon and others to pay the expenses to the CIA and the Cuban operatives to set up the assassination of JFK in three cities. The first city was Chicago on November 2, 1963. The Second city was Tampa on November 20th and the third was Dallas where they finally succeeded in killing Kennedy.

Hoffa's big mouth and making threats to the Mafia bosses about the secret loans they were given to build Las Vegas and Atlantic City from Teamster's pension funds, and he was also threatening Nixon and other government officials about the cover-up of the JFK Assassination made him a marked man. While in federal prison, Hoffa had made another enemy in Raymond Patriarca, mob boss in New England and arch enemy of the Kennedy's. Hoffa confronted Patriarca in Lewisburg Federal Prison and mocked him by saying ha, ha, ha. I got the Kennedy's. Carlos, and Santo and some of those assholes at the CIA got him for me. What happened they hated you worse than me? You could not get to them.

In 1974 Hoffa was warned by many to shut his mouth, and not to try to run for the Leadership of the Teamsters again. Russell Bufalino tried to convince Hoffa two weeks before at a Frank Sheeran awards night in Philly. Frank asked him to stand down and shut his mouth about going to the feds and running for

Teamster's President again. So, a plan was put in place to get rid of Hoffa.

Hoffa's Final Resting Place

My Dad traveled to Lake Orkin Michigan around the 4th of July 1975 to rent a house in the area to prepare for a meeting that was to deal with Jimmy Hoffa and the events. He was making everyone nervous about what had occurred in Dallas in 1963, and numerous other major issues that he supposedly had kept records on the Mob and the Government.

Jimmy wanted to run for the Presidency of the Teamsters again in 1976 and not wait until 1980 as it stated in his pardon from Nixon. It had been rumored from sources that Hoffa, while attempting to gain back control of the Teamsters had provided information to the Feds in exchange for a favorable decision to try and lift his union restrictions.

The whole plan was built around Russell Bufalino's granddaughter's wedding on Aug 1,1975in Detroit, Michigan. A meeting was set up on July 30, where Russell, Hoffa, Tony Pro, Tony Jack and Frank Sheeran would meet to hash out all the issues Hoffa was running around talking about.

The meeting was set up to meet at the Machus Red Fox Restaurant outside of Detroit for 2:30 pm, but plans changed at the last minute. Frank and three others picked Hoffa up at 3pm and drove him to the House my Dad had rented earlier in the month.

When they arrived at the house, Frank and Jimmy went up to the door while the other three guys drove off. Jimmy said" Do you want me to knock?" Half joking. Frank said nah, and they went inside. Frank closed the door and fired two bullets into Hoffa's head. Jimmy fell on the rug, Dad and two other cleaners were inside the house at the time. Frank left without saying a word. The two cleaners rolled up Hoffa's body in a rug and placed it into a body bag. They carried it to the trunk of the car waiting in the garage for my Dad to drive it to a pre-arranged mob connected crematorium in the area.

My Dad drove alone to the crematorium and placed the body in the oven and waited 90 min for the ashes. He then took a container of ashes to Lake Orion where Hoffa had a summer home, and dumped the ashes along the shoreline. When Russell Bufalino put together a plan together with anyone no one person knew the whole plan, not even Frank or Dad. This way no one could rat on the others involved.

The five New York Mob Family's used the Bufalino and Patriarca families to carry out most of the major hit's in the country. They did this to avoid all out wars in NYC, which was always bad for business. This was another instance where Dad was like the "Invincible Man".

In the book "I Heard You Paint Houses", being made into a feature film called "The Irishman". The author talks about the man he called "The Real Estater", in which the name just gave him chills because of his cunning plan to pull off this unsolved crime for over 50 years.

Conspiracy & Coverup

Since November 22,1963 at least 106 people have died under very suspicious circumstances that had some sort of information about the JFK Assassination. Most very incidental about what they had witnessed that day. Strange but true. Early in 1975 the US Senate formed the Church Committee to investigate the JFK Assassination and possible cover up. Shortly before, Church Committee was to hear testimony from Sam Giancana, who was the former boss of Chicago's Mob family, Former Associate of Joseph Kennedy, and power behind the 1960 election in Cook County which gave JFK the state of Illinois and the Presidency.

Giancana was shot in his home on June 19,1975. He was shot by someone he knew with seven shots, one in the mouth, five under the chin, and one to the head. Giancana was shot in this form because he was considered a "Rat".

John Roselli also from Chicago, and had Miami connections to Santo Trafficante Jr. Roselli was found dead on August 9,1975 in Florida. His body was cut in half and put into a 50-gallon drum. Roselli was thought to be the shooter from the "Grassy Knoll" in Dallas that got off the kill shot that killed JFK.

Charles Nicoletti another Chicago hit man, was shot gangland style with three shots to his head as he sat in his car on March 29,1976. Nicoletti also was in Dallas that day. He was said to be in the Dal-Mar Building on the 3rd floor with a rifle and hit Kennedy from behind. The Del-Mar was right across from the book depository building. The Warren report falsely claimed Oswald fired from. Nicoletti was to give the Church Committee testimony soon.

On that same day of March 29,1976 another man associated with Carlos Marcello, Crime boss of New Orleans, named was George de Mohrenschildt was also supposed to testify before the Church Committee, and The House Select Committee on Assassinations. He committed suicide and was found in his home alone.

When the House Select Committee on Assassinations called witnesses again in 1977 they hit a stone wall of death again. Mob boss Joseph Civello in Dallas who was connected to Carlos Marcello, LBJ, and Hoover, was thought to be an informer was found dead in bed with pillow over face.

Carlos Prio, an Anti-Castro Cuban was found with his head blown off on May 5,1977. He was involved with the Bay of Pigs affair, but was called to testify. He may have been in Dallas on that day.

David Sanchez Morales, the undercover CIA scumbag that was the CIA spook that planned everything, from Bay of Pigs for Nixon, and then made sure it failed when JFK became president in 1961. Morales bragged that he was there when both Kennedys were killed. He said in Dallas, “We got the SOB” and was reported to be spotted in LA when RFK was killed and quite possibly the second shooter that got Robert from behind where 22 shots were fired in that hallway. Sir Hans gun fired seven shots. He was later heard bragging, that we got the little prick.

Well on May 8th,1978, Morales died in the hospital from some sort of poisoning. No autopsy was done by his family and he was cremated.

JFK had very serious and powerful enemies in the form of LBJ, George HW Bush, Richard Nixon, J Edgar Hoover, Allen Dulles and Dean Acheson. First and foremost, JFK was not supposed to win in 1960.

Nixon was supposed to be a shoe in, but the mob came through for him to win in Chicago. Nixon was supposed to invade Cuba with an October surprise before the election day. Dulles informed Kennedy, and Bobby let the cat out of the bag to fuck Nixon so he would not have a positive October surprise in invading Cuba. When Kennedy was elected, he attempted Bay of Pigs himself, and CIA and Allen Dulles fucked him and it failed.

The Cabal which Kennedy was not part of, even though he was wealthy, The Mob, the Unions that put him in office, the MIC the Military Industrial Complex, being anti Viet Nam, Cubans from Bay of Pigs, World Banks you name it. They hated him and his brother.

By acting as a truly righteous and just leader despite his own demons which were many, he had fought in World War II and did not want to take America down that road again. JFK had made so many enemies that his assassination was a foregone conclusion. Funny thing, he was aware that it was going to happen. He had dreams about a man on a tall building. he said anyone could do it. He knew about the November 2, 1963 threat at the Army Navy game in Chicago. That is why they cancelled the trip. On his last visit to see his Dad in Hyannis the week before his last trip, he was said to be crying and saying goodbye to his father. He told someone he put it into the hands of "God".

To be perfectly honest here my Dad and Frank Sheeran participated in several of these events of clean up for the Mob. Because it was business. The rest was done by CIA Spooks, you know those little invisible men. If there was a point of no return for JFK, it was he saw US military action in shades of grey, the Dulles Brothers saw only black and white. He still may have survived a second term had he not called out organized crime and the CIA, threatening to destroy both.

The person who knew that better than anyone else was Robert Kennedy. Before leaving office, he made sure every Dulles family member employed by the federal government was fired.

When asked the question who killed JFK, Robert would answer Allen Dulles is the Prime Suspect. The first man JFK fired as Director of the CIA after he was betrayed in the Bay of Pigs Operation. Most believe Dulles old CIA pals is who killed JFK in 1963. Dulles died in 1969 and must be burning in hell, because he was also the banker for the Nazi's along with Prescott Bush during World War II in Switzerland.

They were fined $128,000 for hiding Nazi money in an American bank. Dulles was the founder of the CIA that brought the Nazi's to America after the war to work for CIA.

They only two Conspirators Hierarchy that died natural deaths were Carlos Marcello, who on his deathbed confessed to his involvement, but wished they had not killed Giovanni, meaning JFK. He wished they had killed RFK, because RFK had him deported to Mexico where he was in a jail that was like hell he said. The other Santo Trafficante who admitted to his attorney on his deathbed that he had done it for Jimmy Hoffa, because he kept bugging him and had gave him $350,000 to get the job done.

Big Brother Jerry

I had known Jerry Tillinghast for many years. He was always like a big brother to me. For several years, we played softball four nights a week together on two different teams; for our Employer City of Providence and Smith Hills Polish Social Club. It was at the Polish club one night that Jerry came up to me and gave me an ass chewing. He called me outside and started yelling at me," What are you doing? Do you want to get killed? Because I was sticking up for all my friends.

Jerry said use the brains that I have and make better choices. He said he heard stories about me getting in all sorts of trouble sticking up for my friends. He told me he had heard the story about me spitting in Ronnie Gortere's face when he pulled a gun on me in the Polish Club last week and then I chased him out the door.

He then tells me if he hears any more stories about me, he is going to come back and kick my ass all over the place. Jerry put the fear of God in me. He also showed me a side to him that very few knew from him, because he was the most feared guy in Providence at the time.

He also wanted to know why I wacked three guys with a baseball bat a few nights earlier, defending another friend who could not really defend himself. I told him my friend, Eddy B who had been shot in the head years earlier at the Pizza World. Eddy was outside the club when three guys attacked him. I knew Eddy couldn't defend himself, so I jumped in and helped him out. One of the guys was a cousin of Eddy's, they were arguing when I came outside and smacked the three of them with a baseball bat. Then chased them away while bleeding from their heads.

I found out the next morning that the cops were looking for me, so I went to police station and told them I did not know anything about the event. They put me in a line up in front of the three guys but no one ID me, so that was end of story as far as I was concerned.

The Bonded Vault was Hudson Furs to the public, but to the mob it was their bank. What it amounted to was boxes that were used by all the bookmakers and anyone else that was plugged into the New England Mob. Guys used to gamble all week and on Monday meet at Hudson Furs. The bookmakers would go to their boxes and straighten out their tabs each week. Most would not worry about getting robbed at Hudson furs because Raymond had the place under his protection for over 30 years. As told to me by old friend Chucky Flynn.

One morning around 9am a van pulled up to the door, one guy with a beard got out and walked in with a gun. He told the two men and one woman it was a stick up and placed pillow cases over their heads. six more men entered Hudson furs that morning and went right to work drilling open boxes. It took a couple of hours but this was the biggest robbery in US history.

Several months later there was a trial in which my friend Jerry was charged with taking part in the robbery. Jerry was found not guilty along with two others. Chucky Flynn was found guilty, with two others. It was rumored to be the largest robbery in US History.

John Francis NYC

My Father and Sheeran were involved in several of the most infamous killings in the 70's. They were involved in the Crazy Joe Gallo hit in NYC in 1972, preventing a race war and a mafia war between the five families.

They were involved in the disappearance of James Hoffa in 1975, former head of the Teamster Union. They were involved in the killing of Salvatore "Sally Bugs", who was a witness to the Hoffa case, and was about to turn into a federal witness regarding the Hoffa issue. No one has ever been charged in the Hoffa case, my father also worked for the Patriarca family over the years and was involved with the IRA in the conflict in Northern Ireland. He was arrested numerous times over the years but never did time in prison.

His greatest claim to fame was being invisible. He was there but no one ever saw him there. He learned this from Russell Bufalino who was called the “Quiet Don”. Norman "Scouse" Johnson states in his book “Black Eyes and Blue Blood” John Francis was one of the cleverest men he had ever met in his life, not to mention an extremely shrewd businessman.

John started mixing with the New York underworld, and some of the top guys came to notice what a smart operator he was. He quickly came to the attention of Mobster Russell Bufalino. Who had been accused of ordering the murder of the teamster’s Boss. John introduced Norman to the New York Italian Gangsters as “My Very Good Friend”, which meant that he was one of them and could be trusted implicitly. He took him to meet Russell and Frank Sheeran at an Italian restaurant near Broadway, and said this was very big stuff because Russell was the Godfather.

Norman and Dad were involved in loan sharking and money laundering in the US and Canada and Europe. Norman said John’s financial brilliance provided his family a very prosperous lifestyle. John was always a bit slippery and you could never get a read on him 100%. John was always on the move and had many routes to launder the money for the Bufalino crime family. John was not only Bufalino’s driver from time to time he was also his most trusted associate handling all the cash from legal and illegal business by several mob families.

The authors talk about researching John Francis, and learned he was a Major Associate Member with the Bufalino family in New York and PA, and a very close associate of Frank Sheeran and Jimmy Hoffa.

Norman also discussed one night at a restaurant on 3rd Ave in New York City, when Frank Sinatra came in with his entourage, Sinatra sent a bottle of Dom Perignon champagne over, because he knew John well from being Bufalino's side kick. John said that you never know what mood Frank will be in on any given night, and that he was not a man you could take for granted.

When Norman and John were last together, John was saving a mutual friend's life from being wacked by the Bonanno family. Louis Rush had a contract put on his head because of some shit he had gotten into with the Bonanno's over a shake down this happened in 1978. Well John called Bufalino, who called Bonanno and had the hit called off.

In 1980, John was under a lot of pressure with Bufalino behind bars, even though Russell was still pulling all the strings from jail, but John was being delegated more and more work to do with a lot of other mob family's money which made him very unnerved. And you could tell he wanted out before he got killed himself, because of what he knew about events going back as far as 1951, and having a career that lasted 30 years very rare indeed.

Spruce Street

I was at my job at the highway department one morning when we heard there was a snowstorm headed our way later that night. Everyone was gearing up for it by putting plows and other equipment together for the storm. One of my bosses "Buckles" who happened to be a cousin of mine by marriage, told me to go get three pointed shovels and go drop them off at the Acorn social club on Spruce St. up on Federal Hill. This club was owned by Bobo, who was a major gangster in the Patriarca family.

I delivered the three shovels to the club. Bobo told me to put them in the back room behind the door. I did and said good bye, I left and drove back to public works to wait for the snow to come. I usually worked as an inspector following trucks around, making sure they were doing their jobs plowing Federal Hill, and keeping track of the private contractors who also plowed for the city.

The snow started mid-afternoon, and I was driving my city auto around Federal Hill. At about 9 pm Buckles called me to meet him at the city yard were the big trucks where. When I arrived, he was in the driver's seat of a 10-wheeler, the largest truck the city owned. He told me to follow him to Spruce St. When we arrived at Spruce St. Buckles pulled up on the sidewalk in front of Bobo's Club blocking the whole front of the building which had a large window in front. Buckles got out of the truck, but left it running and came over and got into my auto. He then told me to go to the Federal Grill and have coffee. We went there and sat in there for half hour or so and then received a call on the walkie-talkie radio he had with him.

The call stated we could go back and get the 10-wheel truck at the club now. We would learn later that night from Bobo that he had allegedly killed Dickie C. in the club while the truck was in front of the club protecting the view, and the noise of the six shots he had put into Dickie. He had also hit him with a ball-peen hammer in the forehead that had gotten stuck in the forehead and could not get pulled out. They then rolled Dickie in a rug, put him in a dark van, and drove into Swansea Mass. Where they were going to bury him in the woods.

They drove into the woods but had left snow tracks on the path into the woods. These tracks where seen by a Swansea police officer who was up to no good himself. He had a young lady in his police car, and was about to have a sexual experience with her. He figured he needed to drop her off before he pursued these tire tracks into the woods, since they had found murder victims in this area in the past.

The mobsters in the van had spotted the police auto lights in the distance and panicked. They dropped Dickie's body in the middle of the path with the three shovels and the hammer still stuck in his forehead and drove off, back onto 295 back to Providence.

By the time police officer returned after dropping off the women they were long gone. This was not solved for over ten years when several guys involved ratted on Bobo and then went into the Witness Protection program. Five rats that should drown.

Now, I was also working with Dickie's nephew, also with the city of Providence and I went to funeral parlor with him to view the body in person. Pretty shocking sight.

Raymond and JFK

I had just stopped at the office to say hello to Raymond Patriarca one day, or see if there was something I could do for him regarding my city job type of work. The subject of JFK came up and I could see it gave him grief on some level. He then starts talking about who he calls that little prick Jimmy Hoffa, he says, "You know what Little Prick did to me in the Federal prison in PA"? He came up to me with a crowd around like he wanted to embarrass me. He then goes on to say "Ha, Ha, Santo and Carlos got him for me. What's a matter you could not pull it off? You were no. 1 on their list, they hated you worse than me.

They even got the CIA and the government to cover their ass afterwards. I paid for the whole thing from the pension fund. I did a lot of people a great favor, and now they want me to take a backseat to Fitzpatrick," who was the current President of Teamsters Union. Raymond said, "Fuck you Hoffa get away from me".

Raymond said he knew it was a major conspiracy including people in and out of government, because he knew of three different cities that were involved in the deed. Such as, on Nov 2, 1963, the hit was set up in Chicago by Sam Giancana, some Cubans, and others. I checked this later and found it to be true, but it was stopped because the FBI received info that it would happen at the Army Navy game and Kennedy never traveled there.

The secret service arrested a team of four, three shooters and a guy named Thomas Arthur Valle. Who was a similar guy to Oswald, and would have been set up as the lone gunman the fall guy. The cover-up took it to the next level by charging the secret service agent named Abraham Bolden who had discovered the plot with a crime. Bolden had sent him to prison on a phony drug charge, to shut him up before he could give testimony to Warren Report.

On Nov 20, 1963 in Tampa, Florida, Santo Trafficante Jr. had a team of shooters to try to get Kennedy while he was visiting and riding in a motorcade that was 20 miles long, but changed at the last minute, so an attempt was never made. A Cuban exile named Gilberto Lopez was going to be the lone gunman who was going to be set up.

In Dallas, they had the biggest team and best plan to pull it off. Raymond said there were seven people involved in Dallas and one of them was not Oswald. He was set up as the fall guy. There were four mobsters and three CIA Operatives, and many other government and police involved in the cover up.

One last comment about one of the shooters named David Morales, ex-CIA, ex Bay of Pigs operator, bragged about the fact of the JFK and RFK killings and that he was there for both. Many years later he was arrested as one of Watergate Burglars found inside the office working for Richard Nixon.

There is much more to discuss on this subject. Names included, testimony, deathbed confessions, and multiple murders, of all main players and mob bosses, before they could ever testify in government hearings over the years.

Russell had my Dad bring three long rifles to Chicago in October, and Frank delivered several long rifles to Maryland which they later believed were used in Dallas, and the failed attempt in Chicago at the Army Navy game on November 2, 1963.

PARTY IN NYC

My Father called me from NYC one evening and told me to take a ride to New York City this coming Friday night because they were having a Getting out of jail party at Ruggiero's Restaurant for Uncle Richie Gomes. Richey was a childhood friend of my father.

As a young man, Richey joined a crew of Rhode Island non-Italian mobsters led by Gerard Ouimette, a feared mob enforcer who had strong ties with crime families in Providence, Boston and New York City.

As my Father and his buddy Frank Sheeran were not of Italian descent and were not able to be inducted into the La Cosa Nostra. But they certainly were counted on to do a lot of the dirty deeds that were required. I drove up to NYC that Friday with another friend Kevin H. and we arrived in city at about seven pm and parked on Mulberry St. As we walked in, a big guy walked up to stop us and he asked are you here for the private party because we are closed tonight. I said yes, we are and then I see a familiar face. It was Frank Sheeran, my father's partner in crime who stood 6 ft. 5. He yelled out, "Let them in there with us." Kevin and I were much younger than the crowd of guys in the restaurant.

Frank grabs me and says, "Come here kiddo, I have not seen you in a while. Your father's right over here with Richey, John and the Frenchmen." I was led to the back room of the restaurant where my father was standing and talking to guys at a long table.

I was introduced to several I did not know and several that I had known. Richey Gomes comes and gives me a big hug and kisses me on both cheeks and says, "Hey kid it's been a long time." I laughed and said, "Well stop going to jail and you would see me more." Richie then says, "Here meet the guys; this is my good friend John Gotti. We did some time together, and do you know Gerard?" I said yes, I have met him before, and your Dad's boss Russell Bufalino, and Big Frank you know, and this is your cousin Jimmy Conway.

Several years later Jimmy Conway was made famous in the Movie Good Fella's, where Bobby De Nero played Jimmy Conway in that great film. I met several other big named wise guys and several other guys around the room; it was like a who's who of the Gambino Crime Family in NYC. It was very intimidating for a 25-year-old.

Richie Gomes held a special stature in the Rhode Island and New York underworld. He had been a lifelong friend and driver of John Gotti, the head of the New York based Gambino crime family. In the 60's Gomes, and Gotti struck up a friendship while they both were serving time in the federal penitentiary in Lewisburg, PA. The bond between Richey and the late Gotti grew even stronger, after the murder of Gotti's neighbor who had struck Gotti's young son with his auto and killed the boy.

Gomes was one of the hoods that grabbed the neighbor and threw him in a van and he was never seen alive again. I stayed a few hours at the party bullshitting with my Father, Frank, and Russell. There were about 30 Italian wise guys there, and it was loud as hell. That is not always a good thing when you have a crew of wacky Irishman and loud mouth Italians in the same room. There may be a riot or a shootout with this crowd.

My father has me say goodbye to everyone I had met out of respect, shake hands again, and then him and Frank walk me out to where I parked my car. He gives me a wad of cash and they both hug me and tell me to stay out of trouble. We leave to go back to Providence with my head spinning at what I just experienced.

Richie 'Red Ball' Gomes had spent 50 years of his life behind bars for different crimes, but he died at home in North Providence with 2 photos on the wall, one of Raymond Patriarca and the other of John Gotti. The head of RI state police stated if there was a Mob Hall of Fame Richey Gomes would be in it.

Bulger Beatdown

One Friday evening Kevin Hanrahan and I were out drinking and making the rounds around Smith Hill and stopped at the 350 Club on Chalkstone Ave.

When we walked in there were five or six guys in there. It was about closing time and everyone was drunk and shitfaced. At the end of the bar there were three guys I had never seen before. One of them was Whitey Bulger, a big-time hood from Boston who worked for Raymond Patriarca. The same mob boss that my father worked for and was close friends with.

Well Kevin knew Bulger from Boston. Bulger yells out to Kevin. "I heard people are taking pot shots at you these days, you must be getting soft!" Several weeks earlier Kevin had been shot five times in a bar on Federal Hill, and did not seek medical attention or tell police who had shot him. Well Kevin says, "Fuck You Whitey", and cracks him in the head with a pool stick and knocked him to the floor. He then kicked him in the head several more times, until he was out the door. He then grabs him and tosses him on the sidewalk.

Whitey's two friends tried to come to his rescue to no avail, because I smacked both with the blackjack I always carried. They were bleeding like pigs right away, and whining and crying as they were thrown outside on sidewalk also. Between Kevin, I and other friends, we played football with their heads on the sidewalk. Then we heard the cops are coming, and we took off fast so as not to be arrested.

Bulger complained to Raymond Patriarca about what happened that night and wanted to whack Kevin and Me for giving him a beatdown, but he had to get Raymond's permission to do anything in New England and especially in Providence.

Well a couple of weeks later Kevin and I were called to a restaurant on Atwells Ave up on Federal Hill for a Sit Down, where all parties are called in to settle problems before any more shit happened.

Raymond Patriarca, Nicky Bianco, Russell Bufalino, Frank Sheeran, and my Dad were there for me and Kevin. Bulger was there with three guys also, and to make a long story short, Bulger was told he was at fault for coming down to Providence and starting shit and insulting Kevin. He was told to move on and that we were untouchable. If something happened to us they would be at war with New York and Providence Mob family's. Kevin and I had to promise that it was over and would not start anymore shit.

I was sweating bullets and was very thankful for those guys standing up for me. There would be two more occurrences where Bulger and I crossed paths over the years. He always had a remark about me hanging with the Italians in Providence.

My Dad never liked Bulger, thought he was a piece of shit, and suffered from little man's disease, and always had a chip on his shoulder. There were always rumors that he was a "Rat", which turned out to be true many years later, when it came out he was a FBI informant for 30 years. He killed at least 19 Men and Women as a Confidential Informant for the Boston FBI. He was sentenced to 9 life sentences in 2015.

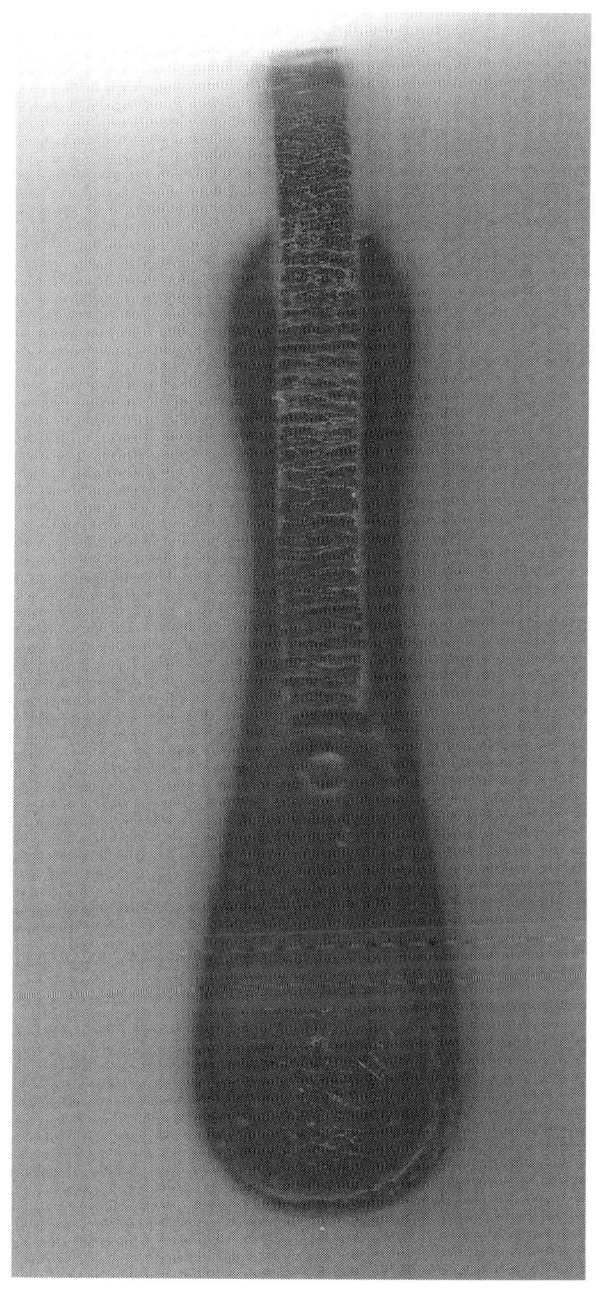

Blizzard of 1978

The Blizzard of 1978 became the storm of the century when hundreds of lives were lost. High winds over 85 mph slammed the state and over four feet of snow fell in Rhode Island. On February 5, 1978, it started to snow in Rhode Island. It was a Sunday and the storm was coming up the east coast very slowly so we received just a dusting overnight.

Working in public works and getting called in on a Sunday to plow snow or be an inspector on snow routes was considered gravy time, or golden time. We received double time regarding our hourly wages. I was called in to work at noon on the 5th to ride shotgun on a plow truck and sander up on the east side hills of Providence.

Buckles and Blackjack oversaw the snowplowing of city trucks, and for calling in private contractors to assist the city in snow removal. They were paid by the hour at a rate of $45 an hour at the time.

Monday the weather forecast got worse. The storm had merged with another weather system around Washington DC and now had winds up to 85 miles an hour like a tropical hurricane and was heading right for us.

They had not cancelled school on Monday or closed any businesses. I remained on duty all night. Now it was Monday and the snow was starting to stick and accumulate several inches an hour by noon on Monday.

Shortly after noon on Monday the reports from New York were very bad especially from Long Island, which is at the top of Narragansett Bay, and downtown Providence is at the mouth of the Bay. So, at noon time all hell broke loose, TV and radio stations were telling everyone the schools were being released and businesses would be closing earlier, all of which was the worst thing they could have done.

In the next 24 hours, 28 inches of snow came down on Rhode Island. At least 12 inches in the first six hours causing the worst traffic jam on 95 and 195 and every Main Street or side road in the state.

Back at Public Works we were calling in every employee and private contractor that we could get in, which was not many because there were not any passable roads. Even the plow trucks could not get out plowing because so many autos were stuck everywhere.

Cars and trucks were stopped dead in their tracks on 95, trapping thousands on their way home from work or school with their children. Matter of fact my son Jay was picked up by a policeman friend of mine along with his own son from school. They had to sleep in a firehouse for two nights before my friend could carry them home.

The snow was 4ft high, with 80 mile an hour winds, the drifts went up to window levels on 3rd floor houses. This went on for four days, until the Army Corp of Engineers came and rescued the state with plows that were 25 feet tall. I was on duty for eight days and did not get home until the 6th day. During those eight days,

I saw and witnessed events I never dreamed I would see in America.

Over 100 people died on the roads stranded in their auto on the interstates, highway and small side roads within vision of their homes but could not get there. Bodies were being dragged on sleds from hospitals to the morgues.

With an event like this it was the biggest moneymaking opportunity for Cianci and his cronies. Also for us at Public works where we were on the clock at double time for over a week. If I remember well, Buckles put my time in and my pay was over $10,000 for the week and $8000 take home which turned into a windfall when I retired 10 years later and my pension was based on 1978 income.

Sally Bugs and Napo

On March 21, 1978, my father and Frank Sheeran participated in a hit that was attached to the Jimmy Hoffa killing. There were headlines on TV and in newspapers across the country about a murder that occurred in NYC in broad daylight on Mulberry St in the Little Italy section of New York. The victim was Salvatore "Sally Bugs"

"Sally Bugs" was the mobster who drove the auto that took Jimmy Hoffa to the house where he met his death several years earlier. It was mid-afternoon on a sunny day on Mulberry St in NYC, and the location was close to the restaurant that I had attended for Richey Gomes a few months earlier with my father, Frank, John Gotti, Jimmy Conway, and Russell Bufalino.

My father and Frank Sheeran were sitting in a parking space across from the social club waiting for Sally Bugs to arrive as he did on most days to take care of business at the club.

When they spotted him, they pull up and parked on the side street. They got out of the stolen auto they were in and walked up to Sally Bugs as he got out of his auto. Frank said hello Sal and Sal responded Hi Irish. Then Sal looked over at my Dad, who he did not know, and looked like he was waiting for an intro to my dad when Frank raised his gun and shot Sal several times in the head. Then my father shot Sal once in the chest to make sure Sal would not get up behind his auto in the gutter. Several witnesses were yelling, screaming and diving behind autos and buildings, but no one came out of the social club.

My Father and Frank returned to the stolen car where my Father drove and Frank got in the passenger seat and drove off as if nothing had just occurred.
Generally, Frank would go by himself and do the shooting leaving my father in the car, to just drive away, on this day my father got out of the auto to cover Frank in the event someone else might come outside from the social club to defend Sally Bugs.

At the time of his killing, "Sally Bugs" was thought to be talking to the Feds about the Hoffa murder. Also about the murder of Anthony Castellitto, which took place in 1961. Tony (Pro) enlisted "Sally Bugs" to kill

Anthony Castellitto. Sally was under indictment for the Castellitto murder when Frank and my Dad took him out.

April 12, 1978, Joseph Napolitano, a member of the Patriarca crime family, was convicted of trying to distribute $3.3 million in counterfeit $100 bills, but was released on bail pending sentencing in October.

During his trial one of his defenses was that he was an FBI informant. Raymond Patriarca was not going to wait for the other shoe to fall, and get indicted himself for the $100 bills. Raymond called my father who was still up in the NYC area. Napolitano was said to be hiding out somewhere in Brooklyn under FBI protection.

My father told me they had been watching a certain house for several days, and discovered that Napolitano was not under FBI protection. But he left early each morning to go to his business, but came home at 4:30 pm each day. Even though Dad stated Napolitano was not under the Fed's thumb, Patriarca still wanted him gone.

Several months later, on September 6, 1978 the hit was carried out. My Dad and two others with masks were sitting back 100 yards or so from the driveway in a van, waiting for him to bring his car to a halt and turn off the engine. When he did the two men jumped out before Joe could reach for a gun or respond in anyway. They stood there and blasted away. One shotgun blast tore half of Joe's face off, the second blast took his head off. The two guys jumped back in the van as quick as they had jumped out and they were gone into traffic.

The scene that played out that day gave my father nightmares and he made up his mind that he couldn't do this no more. He said he counted his blessings that he was alive, never done time in prison and was sick of death and wanted to somehow have a normal life back in RI.

I saw it in my father eyes and knew that the hit really shook him up. A change was needed for him to remain alive in this world. He knew he could be him next, because of all the deeds he did and knew about. He also thought about the freedom he came to enjoy because he seen guy's going in and out of jail. Stand Up Guy's one moment, Rat's the next. He always said jail was not for him.

God Fathers Meeting

It was a hot day in June 1978, I was working on the emergency truck for City of Providence with Anthony Melise. We received a call from dispatch telling us that I was wanted up at "The Office" which was Raymond Patriarca's business National Cigarette Machine and Coin-o Matic.

We arrive and there is a big black Lincoln limo in the side alley near the back of the building. There are several men standing outside the auto. One is my Dad the others are Raymond, Russell, and another man in a fedora with sunglasses on.

Raymond calls me over and says your Dad tells me you have some info on a couple trailers full of cigarettes. I tell him I have been working part time for RJ Reynolds cigarettes handing out free cigs in Springfield and Providence at night, outside clubs with models. I told him that I knew where they have two tractor trailers full of cigarettes and were they parking them down the shipyard. Also, I have the truck plate numbers and other info on the truck.

Dad and Russell come over to me and give hugs and kisses on both cheeks, they turn and introduce me to Santo Trafficante the other man in the fedora and sunglasses, Santo is the mob boss of Tampa and Miami.

We stood there outside bullshitting for a few minutes about me looking like my old man, saying the apple does not fall to far from the tree with you kiddo.

I then hand Raymond the sheet of paper with the trailer info on it, He then says if all goes well this will be your biggest payday. Several days later received a call from model agency, that there will be no work until further notice. The truckload of cigs had disappeared.

Watch Hill Weekend

Watch Hill RI is an exclusive summer resort community with a strong sense of privacy and discreetly used wealth. Which makes it one of the greatest unknown treasures in America. Which is why my Dad invited Russ, Frank, and myself to his beach house on the Labor Day Weekend in 1978.

This would be the last time the three of them would be together before Russ and Frank would be sent away to Federal Prison. On Conspiracy charges for crimes the Fed's had been hounding them for several years since Hoffa's disappearance in July of 1975.

I arrived on Friday afternoon before anyone else and found Dad sitting in a beach chair alone watching the waves crash along the shore of the bay. He was sitting there in a trance with a beer cooler next to him. I could see something was different today as he just kept looking out at the waves crash on the shoreline. I asked What's going on? You alright? He said Yea. Sit down grab a beer. I asked what you thinking about? He says just sitting here playing a tape of my life in my head like it was a bad movie. Starting all the way back to the PT boats in the pacific many moons ago, and how I survived and why I survived.

I am feeling guilty about all the shit I have done along the way to you and your sister and others. I said forget about it we all survived for the most part. He said that don't make it right, I know that shooting at the Pizza World in 1968 fucked your head for real. You ended up quitting school and throwing basketball away. You could at least have gone on to play at Providence College and got your education. Instead you end up in Nam three years later and all fucked up in the head.

That was all on me. The shooter wanted to get back at me for some shit that happened 20 years earlier. And that's just the start of it, never mind all the stuff I been involved in over the years. Russ, and Frank, may now be going away because of that Hoffa shit. That's why we are getting together it may be the last time we all get to sit down in same place. The Doctor told me my cancer popped back up and I needed to be treated again. That's why I am going down memory lane in my head. I told him you are going to be alright, you are a miserable prick who will outlive all of us. Look in the mirror smartass he says; the apple does not fall to far from the tree Jr. We then walked back up to the house to get dressed to go out for a lobster dinner down at the pier.

Frank and Russ arrived the next morning at about ten in a Black Caddy smoking big cigars and wearing loud flowery shirts and straw hats looking like clowns never mind gangsters. We greeted them in the driveway with hugging and kissing on both cheeks. It's an Italian thing, just a way of showing respect. Frank yells out "what is this the Kennedy Compound Bull". Dad says yea I rented just for you guys because you are royalty. Frank says were royalty alright, the Feds are about to give us two penthouse suites up at the big house in Danbury.

Russ says enough of that shit, let's enjoy the weekend. Frank grabs me in a headlock and says you staying out of trouble 'Kiddo'. Russ and Frank both give out hearty laughs about me staying out of trouble, Russ says it's his middle name. Don't you know that, He is the spit from his father's mouth and they never stay out of trouble it just seems finds them. enough already, let's have a beer. We all go in the house laughing away.

Later that evening sitting outside overlooking Narragansett Bay in all its beauty around a campfire, Dad had started the fire an hour earlier, we just started shooting the shit about how they had met each other many years ago.

Russ let's out a big laugh and says I met these two Micks way back in the 1950s when they were still wet behind the ears. I met your Dad when he was running errands for Meyer Lansky in NYC and Miami. And he was trying to learn 'Yiddish' to impress Meyer. We all laughed because your Dad with that Boston accent going for him he could barely speak English. Well Meyer liked him and trusted him so he told me to take him under my wing and your Dad has been the best driver I ever had.

Except in 1958 at Appalachian he could not get me away from the Feds and we both were arrested running around the woods like dogs. What a fucking day that was huh Bull. Dad says Yea one for the ages, the raid made front page news all over the world.

Frank the big lug was broken down on side of the road driving a tractor trailer truck for some independent company that left him stranded out there. I helped him get it started and gave him my number and told him I would get him started with the Teamsters where he could make good money.

Frank then tells me all the shit he went through in the war spending 440 days in Europe with Patton. I knew he was a tough guy so I hooked him up with Hoffa who needed a tough guy who was not intimidated easy to run errands for him, the rest is history in that regard.

The three of them went on reminiscing about their greatest regret of having to take Jimmy Hoffa down. All three of them were very fond of Jimmy and really loved his family but Jimmy was just to head strong, he would not listen to anyone and thought he was untouchable, because of what he knew and the records he had kept all those years.

After all JFK was not the only president killed that year. South Viet Nam President and his family was also killed by the CIA a few months before JFK. No one is untouchable that is why they carried out the order giving by much higher uppers than Russell, or they would have been killed themselves.

Dad told me to go in the house and get the black satchel on his bed, I went and got the bag and handed it to him. Dad looked in the satchel and said this is what Jimmy died for and what the Feds are looking for and will always be looking for "Hoffa Diary's". All his bullshit records on everyone from the Bay of Pigs, Nixon, Bush, LBJ and Teamsters Pension Fund loans and all the way down to the three of us and what we did for him over the years.

Dad said, "Let's end this bull shit right now" he then stands up and empty's the satchel into the bonfire right in front of us and then throws the leather satchel in the fire to burn to ashes.

On September 28,1978, Russell was arrested for conspiracy, at his trial he was convicted and sent to Federal prison for four years. Frank was also convicted of extortion and sentenced to five years.

Major Hit in NYC

In 1979, Carmine Galante was the man behind the biggest drug connections in US history. The French Connection and The Pizza Connection were his way to get heroin into the country. During the 1970's Galante allegedly organized the murders of eight members of the Gambino crime family, whom he had an intense rivalry with to take over the massive drug trafficking of heroin in the US.

The New York Crime Family were alarmed at Galante's brazen attempt to withhold all the profits from other families. Although he was aware of his many enemies, he said, "No one would dare to kill me." Well in the summer of 1979, the Mafia Commission orders his execution and the plan was put in motion.

Galante was probably the most feared man in NYC. He was thought to have had killed over 80 men himself and another 200 by his associates who had been brought in from Italy and they were called Zips, who were his hit men who also ran his pizza restaurants where the heroin was ran through.

My father was told to go see Aniello Dellacroce the underboss of the Gambino Family who also was John Gotti's mentor and a much-respected man in the Mafia. My father met with O'Neil at an airport parking lot. Where it was very loud so not to be heard by the feds or anyone else that followed O'Neil. O'Neil said he had a job that he wanted him to drive for a major hit soon in Brooklyn, he would need two hot autos, station wagons or large four door sedans. His job would be to drive three guys to a restaurant. Were they will be loaded-very heavy and everyone included Dad were to wear ski masks, there will be many witnesses and lots of publicity because it's Galante.

He also told Dad to be carrying heavy himself to cover anyone coming out of restaurant, Galante has two big bodyguards who are in on it and should behave so just let them walk away.

On July 12,1979, my father and three other guys drive in a station wagon to Joe and Mary's Italian Restaurant on Knickerbocker Ave in Brooklyn. This was a small narrow restaurant with a small patio out back that was fenced in and very isolated. At 3pm or so my father pulls up to front of restaurant quickly puts it in park they all have ski masks on.

My father gets out as the three guys go inside quickly and head to the rear patio where they are sure that Carmine Galante will be. He is there with two others, a friend and the owner of the restaurant. The three fired with shotguns and handguns and all three died instantly. Galante's body guards just walked away. The three shooters ran out jumped in auto, Dad drove several blocks to where they had the second auto, and drove off in a sedan to somewhere near JFK airport. Galante's death photo show him with a cigar in his mouth.

This event was one of my father's last participation in a hit that was a major story. My dad was never questioned regarding this and never saw any of those guys again. In his mind, it was like it never happened, just another day at work. That's how he dealt with it, till many years later when he spoke to me to get it off his chest, because at that point he knew that I knew his background and that nothing would surprise or scare me off.

I knew he regretted all the bad stuff he did for many years. Against many different people and I know now he was trying to get ready for his own death. Meet his maker and was starting to second guess himself and for first time.

He did not have Frank and Russ around anymore, were they knew they always could put a solid plan together and always had each other's backs. He knew many Italians would rat on anyone that would keep them out of jail, the Gallente hit brought a lot of heat in NYC

Dad's Return Home

Around 1979 my father returned to Rhode Island, he knew he still had to make money and got involved in bookmaking. Conventional wisdom is that bookmaking is the mobs bread and butter. To some extent that is true and people's desire to bet on a sporting event is always there.

Back then we didn't have the internet to send bets through Las Vegas so it had to be done illegally. Each week millions of dollars would be bet on some game of chance, and you almost never have a chance of winning. At least with a ball game you have a 50/50 chance of winning.

My father had to get permission from The Office, from Raymond or Nicky to start bookmaking on his own in Providence. He could only do it in certain places because Providence had Jewish, Irish, Italian, Portuguese, and Black bookies in every area of Providence. We started out on the secondary level where independent bookies would lay off large bets, bets that they could not cover without going belly up if they had a bad day, the ultimate backers were Raymond and the Mob.

We took bets on baseball, and basketball, some horse racing and of course the daily lottery. The lottery was called a racial slur, back in those days towards the blacks. We had bookies in Smith Hill, Fox Point, Federal Hill, Warwick, and several in South Providence.

Each bookie handled around 15 clients and they would get 25% cut of all their action. We had a great reputation because everyone knew my Dad had a great connection to The Office, we were always full in terms of the number of layoffs we could take on and how much we could take on to cover large bets.

This was all before cell phones and computers so it was my job most of the time to keep written records. I could not keep all the action in my head, I would fuck it up and be in a lot of shit with the old man. I'd keep records and on Monday morning when we would do all our slips for the previous week. Sunday was the end of the week for us unless Monday night football was in season. I would burn any written records of the previous week's bets.

My Dad got a real job at the Providence Journal as night security guard, Dad took the job to keep the IRS off his back. It was partly because the journal workers were some of biggest gamblers in the city, and he had a lot of connections there. My Dad also remarried a woman who had five children, a ready- made family. It was a strange relationship but who am I to say anything. He settled down, did his bookings, and watched his Red Sox and other sports, which is what he and I always discussed. I don't remember talking about much else unless I had gotten myself in a legal jam in which I needed his help or cash.

He very seldom visited my house maybe ten times over the ten years, when he did it was in and out in less than half hour. He did that everywhere and to everyone, he was always early for every event. This rubbed off on me also even though I had never lived with him past the age of five. We both had ants in our pants as they say. I'll give him this also, Dad never spent more than two nights in jail over the years. He never got caught doing the deeds he was involved in. He had a lot of connections everywhere on both side of the law.

All said he was a Standup guy which is the greatest compliment that can be given to a man, something else that has rubbed off on me and one major reason I am still alive today, trust and respect is the foundation of a man in this world that we lived in.

Shylocking is one of the businesses my Dad participated in. Big money was made from shylocking because, unless the borrower paid everything back in full on top of the 10% juice weekly, and this very seldom happened. It would amount to 500-1000% a year with a never end in sight. Because if you were desperate enough to go to a Shylock and agree to pay that much interest it was doubtful that you could ever repay the whole loan amount back.

It was a cash cow for him and a no-win situation for the borrower. Since paying the exorbitant interest was much better than the consequences for not paying. Like the one time I had to visit a guy, for late payments to my Dad. The guy who owned a house painting company avoided making his weekly payments and was not returning calls. His name was Billy, He used to hang on Smith Hill in one of a dozen or so bars in the Irish area of Providence.

One Friday night me and a friend who I could trust to watch my back and scare the shit out of other people. We enter the bar on Smith Street and spot Billy down at the very end of the bar. He spots me right away and starts waving me over and telling me he has a payment for Dad, I said to him as of today you owe three and I want them all. He starts making excuses so I grabbed him and led him into men's room. Dailey followed me in there also and grabbed Billy from the back, I grabbed his right arm and leaned it over the iron sink and then struck his right hand numerous times with my blackjack breaking his hand and wrist. He was screaming in pain trying to get his money out of his right pants pocket. I finally grabbed the wad of money out of his pants and counted out $450, which was the three payments he owed and put the rest back in his pocket. Warned him not to pull this shit again or both arms would be broke. How are you going to paint if that happens Billy? Dailey and I walked out of the bar in dead silent, we never had heard an Irish bar that quiet.

A short time later my father was having a problem with his auto, so he had it towed to a service station to have it looked at. When the hood was raised in the service department by Ralph a friend of my father, six sticks of dynamite were wired to the front wall of the auto. They were not connected to the battery, my father looked on this as a warning. My father grabbed the six sticks and threw them in trunk in disgust. He knew there were a lot of rats in Providence and NYC that may have talked about some of the stuff he was involved in the past. He never did get to the bottom of who was behind the dynamite he just took it as a warning to make sure he never, "Told Any Tales out of School" as he used to say. From that point on he popped the hood each time got into an auto and checked it out with his little flashlight.

Hoffa Hearing in PA.

Another occurrence happened in August of 1982, my father asks me to take a ride with him to Scranton PA. This was a hearing that he needed to go to for some crime commission. The commission was looking into Russell Bufalino's involvement in numerous things over the years. Frank Sheeran was being brought in from Danbury Federal Prison also to testify.

We arrived at this courthouse and were told to meet with a lawyer retained by Russell to represent my father in the hearing. It was an open meeting not like a grand jury where your lawyer could not go in and represent you. We meet the lawyer and he takes us outside to talk and he tells my dad they will be calling him after Russell gets done testifying. Which may be quick because he will be taking the 5th and not answering many questions either. He advised my Dad to say his name, date of birth, where he works or gets a pension from and not to lie because they know that you know Russell and Frank, and others and that you worked for the Teamsters and ran errands for Jimmy Hoffa. And if they ask you anything else you take the 5th. Okay sounds good to me the old man said. They made us stay in the long hallway outside the hearing room until it was our turn to go in.

Suddenly people are clearing out of courtroom, news guys taking photos of Russell and his lawyers, as he attempts to leave court house. Somehow my Dad and Russell spot each other and they move to greet each other, they hug and kiss each other on the right cheeks and talk for a minute or so under their breath very softly. Russell spots me standing close by and says, "Hello Kiddo, how are you?" "You are keeping an eye on your dad now?" God knows someone has too, I responded yes, "I am keeping him on the straight and narrow." And then Russell says to me, "I hope your keeping your nose clean yourself, you don't need to be involved in all this shit, look where it got us, I am on my way back to prison. Make an honest man of your old man will ya kid?". We hug and kiss each other out of respect. This was the last time I ever saw Russell.

My dad and I and his lawyer go into hearing room filled with people staring at us, the lawyer and my dad go right up front and I sit in first row right behind them. They make my dad swear to tell the truth oath and he does. They ask him to state his name he states, John Francis Sullivan. They ask, "Do you also go by the name of John Francis?" he replies, my name is John Francis Sullivan so that covers the John Francis name does it not?" They ask, "Are you also called The Red Head? My father looks at the lawyer to see if he should respond, lawyer nods his head yes, "Well regarding the red head thing I often wear my Red Sox hat so I've been known to be called the red head. Regarding the John Francis thing my name is John Francis Sullivan." the state's lawyer knows my dad's busting his balls now. He then asks, "Do you know Russell Bufalino and Frank Sheeran?". My dad says, "Yes they are good friends for 20 years or so". "Did you know Jimmy Hoffa?" He again said, "Yes, also a friend from the teamster union where I worked for many years and I used to run errands sometime for Jimmy." From one union office to another. From that point on my father took the fifth at least 30 times to questions about Hoffa disappearance and Frank Sheeran and Russell's business dealing.

They allowed my dad to leave the courthouse telling him that he may be called back and he just waved his hand saying okay. We did not get to see Frank

Sheeran who we were told was going to testify the next day. Being called to this hearing set my dad off to a bad place or bad mood. We drove back to Rhode Island that night and on the way my dad wanted a few beers so I was driving and he was quiet but he was throwing down the beers, and when we arrived at his beach house in Narragansett RI. He wanted to go in his favorite bar for a few more and before we knew it he was bombed.

I start to help him out and he gets angry like I had never seen him before and he is getting physical with me. He starts slapping me in the face 10-12 times as we are walking to the auto, he wanted me to hit him and he kept pushing me and pushing me until he seen me crying and saying I won't hit you because I love you and suddenly like he sobered up and said, "I guess my mother raised you well because you proved to me tonight, you're a real man." He then gave me a bear hug that almost killed me and allowed me to get him in the house.

EPILOGUE

I will make this short and sweet and very direct to those who have read my novel, this was the "Greatest Conspiracy in History". And there was the "Greatest Cover-up" to the "Overthrow of the Greatest Democratic Government in the History of the World". This has happened in many places around the world, but founding fathers never dreamed it could happen in America.

The Cleanup was easy the Cia and the Mob had plenty of experience at completing their mission of eliminating over a hundred people over the years, that had any knowledge of Assassination.

A lot of the info in this book can be found in the Library of Congress in Washington DC. I spent a week verifying the story's info that was told to me over the years, I found most of the info in the Church Senate Hearings records, and Select House Committee on Assassinations records.

We in America need to correct history good or bad so we can learn from our mistakes. So as not to repeat history, "Because of Greed".

One final note about the mystery of the death and disappearance of Jimmy Hoffa and the FBI constant chasing of their tale every time someone says they know where he is buried over the last 42 years. The FBI has continued this because of the chance that they will find Hoffa's satchel of ledgers of the evidence he had collected over the years on everyone including the United States Government at the highest level including the Executive Branch, Judicial, Legislative Branch, and Organized Crime in America.

What occurred on November 22,1963 was the darkest hour in American History. This is my attempt to pull back the curtain and let everyone see what really goes on behind the backs of the "Citizens of the Greatest Nation in the History of Mankind".

Future Novels and Subject Matters

This novel takes us to the late 70s or so and in crime and corruption in Rhode Island that is like the days of Adam and Eve. I was present for Buddy's first term and the crime and the corruption at public works, city hall,tax office, and trash strikes. Murder and mayham up Federal Hill and Smith Hill. The Feds and the State Troopers are everywere. Buddy takes a short vaction then comes back better than ever, and rebuilds downtown Providence.

My next novel will discuss Buddy's first term of Mayor of Providence. We also will discuss my growing up on Smith Hill and Federal Hill and all the wacky and crazy people I grew up with. Smith HILL Tap tales and Knight St adventures with guys shooting crap.Friends Jerry, George, Buckles, and Kevin H . Chief Justices and other corrupt politicians of which Rhode Island had in abundence getting arrested. Lot's of people going to jail.

As Raymond LS Patriarca once told me up at the "Office" on Atwells Ave . " Everyman has a price you just have to find out what it is".

Made in the USA
Monee, IL
04 May 2020

28807209R00067